FERNS

OF

NEW ZEALAND

LAWRIE METCALF

First published in 2003 by New Holland Publishers (NZ) Ltd
Auckland • Sydney • London • Cape Town

218 Lake Road, Northcote, Auckland, New Zealand
14 Aquatic Drive, Frenchs Forest, NSW 2086, Australia
86-88 Edgware Road, London W2 2EA, United Kingdom
80 McKenzie Street, Cape Town 8001, South Africa

www.newhollandpublishers.com

Copyright © 2003 in text: Lawrie Metcalf
Copyright © 2003 in photography: Lawrie Metcalf
Copyright © 2003 New Holland Publishers (NZ) Ltd

Publishing manager: Renée Lang
Design and typesetting: Julie McDermid
Editor: Brian O'Flaherty

Metcalf, L. J. (Lawrence James), 1928-
A photographic guide to ferns of New Zealand / Lawrie Metcalf.
Includes bibliographical references and index.
ISBN 1-877246-94-8
1. Ferns–New Zealand–Identification. 2. Ferns–New Zealand–
Pictorial works. I. Title.
587.30993–dc 21

Colour reproduction by PICA Colour Separation, Singapore
Printed by Times Offset (M) Sdn Bhd, Malaysia

10 9 8 7 6 5 4 3 2 1

Front cover photograph: umbrella fern (*Sticherus cunninghamii*).
Back cover photograph: coastal hardfern (*Blechnum durum*).
Spine photograph: crook or crozier of mamaku (*Cyathea medullaris*).
Title page photograph: mamaku (*Cyathea medullaris*).

Contents

When at high school, I was first introduced to the fascinating world of New Zealand ferns by my friend Geoff Harrow. From that time, native ferns became my first and enduring love in the plant kingdom, and it is hoped that this book might encourage other young New Zealanders to similarly develop an interest in this wonderful part of our New Zealand flora.

Introduction

This guide includes not only the true ferns but also some closely related plants commonly known as fern allies. In New Zealand ferns occur in great abundance, especially the tree ferns, and so it is no wonder that this country is justifiably known as a fern paradise. With almost 200 native species they occur in all manner of situations from salt-splashed coastal rocks to alpine regions, and from moist rainforest to dry scrublands and sunny rocks. In practically all parts of the country, apart from in the dry eastern areas of both islands, ferns comprise a prominent and distinctive feature of the vegetation. With such a wealth of ferns occurring in most parts of the country it was quite natural that the silver fern (*Cyathea dealbata*) became New Zealand's national emblem.

Ferns have an ancient genealogy dating back for over five hundred million years – long before the flowering plants evolved. Unlike flowering plants, ferns have neither flowers nor seeds but reproduce by means of spores. The spores are produced in minute, stalked capsules known as sporangia. In some primitive species (*Leptopteris*) the sporangia are just scattered over the undersurfaces of the fronds, but in the majority of species they are grouped, on the undersurfaces, in clusters of special spore cases known as sori. Generally, they are quite conspicuous on the fronds of most ferns. In fact, the shape and positioning of the sori are some of the main characters used for classifying and identifying ferns. The nature of the veining on the fronds is another character.

The characters that botanists use for classifying the different ferns into various families and genera are not always well defined and, depending upon the views of individual botanists, this may result in many ferns being frequently reassigned to different families and genera.

A question that many novices might well ask, is 'What constitutes a fern?' Some ferns are quite obvious and readily recognised as such, but there are others that do not fit into the typical fern mould. In general, ferns are characterised by having coiled immature fronds (leaves) that uncoil as they develop. These uncoiling fronds are usually known as 'crooks', 'crosiers', or 'fiddle-heads', and they have also been the inspiration for the koru pattern that is frequently used in Maori art. The variations in the branching of vein patterns, on the mature fronds, are also used for identification, while the size, shape and positioning of the sori (spore-producing organs) are usually important. On most species the sori are on the undersurfaces of the fronds, but on some they may be placed around the margins of the fronds or at the tips of the frond segments.

The fern allies described in this guide are the clubmosses (*Lycopodium*) and the fork ferns (*Tmesipteris*). They are even more primitive than ferns and have a much longer fossil history. These fern allies have quite a different appearance to ferns but reproduce in a similar manner, by spores.

Some of the clubmosses superficially resemble true mosses but have their spore cases aggregated into conspicuous, club-like cones or strobili (hence their common name). On one or two species they are not as conspicuous and appear more as a thickening at the tips of the stems. In some areas clubmosses are also a conspicuous part of the vegetation.

The fork ferns are so named because of the manner in which their fertile leaves are forked, so that they appear to be in pairs. Their spore cases are produced on the upper surface of the leaf, in the fork. They are not as common as the clubmosses and mainly occur in moist forests, usually as epiphytes on the trunks of tree ferns. The fork ferns are interesting because their ancestors are said to have been the first plants to produce lignin, the substance which ultimately allowed plant stems to become rigid and woody.

Acknowledgements

Geoff Davidson, Oratia Native Plant Nursery; Lisa Forester, Department of Conservation, Whangarei; Chris Adams, Kaikohe; Edith Shaw, Nelson; and Shannel Courtenay, Department of Conservation, Nelson, all very willingly helped me to locate many fern species photographed for this book, and their assistance is gratefully acknowledged.

How to use this book

In order to assist users to identify the plants illustrated, a simple key has been provided on pages 16–17. At first glance it may appear to be complicated, but with a little practice you should find that it is quite easy to use. Instructions for the key are on page 15.

Headings

Although common names are highlighted, for ease of reference all species described are listed according to their scientific names so that their affinities, with related species, may more easily be seen. The scientific names are those in current use although, given the rather frequent changes to fern names, it is quite possible that some names may well be superseded within a short space of time. The common names given are those that are generally recognised. Some species do not have recognised common names and the temptation to use pretentious, coined names has been resisted. Both common names and scientific names are listed in the index. The family to which each species belongs is also given. Family names appear in the coloured tab at the top margin of each page.

The ferns and allied plants described

Most of the ferns and fern allies described, and illustrated, are the commoner species that are more likely to be seen when journeying around the New Zealand countryside. There are one or two exceptions that have been included because of their interest and because they illustrate the wonderful diversity of the fern world.

All are listed according to their various families. They are in currently accepted botanical order, while the members of each family (genus and species) are grouped together so that it is possible to compare them with related species. The genera and species of each family are arranged in alphabetical order.

When attempting to identify a fern or fern ally in the wild, firstly try to do so with the aid of the key, and then compare it with the description and accompanying illustration. Each description gives the main characters necessary for identifying the particular species. Some are quite obvious and may be identified from the illustration alone, while others may also need to be checked against the description. For final confirmation, check it against the distribution map.

Terminology

In all descriptions an attempt has been made to keep botanical terminology to a minimum, but it is not always possible to completely avoid the use of such terms. In some instances it is for greater accuracy, and in others to avoid using wordy phrases that may be better expressed by just one word.

With ferns being so different from flowering plants it is necessary that readers become familiar with some of the main terms that are used to describe them. Most of these terms relate to their fronds. The basal portion of a fern (including the root system) is known as the **rhizome**. A fern frond usually consists of a stalk known as the **stipe** (plural stipes), and a leafy portion known as the **blade** or lamina. The blade may have continuous, uncut margins, in which case it is known as **simple** (refer to *Pyrrosia*), or it may be divided into lobes or segments. The fronds of a fern such as *Microsorum pustulatum* are usually **lobed**, and are referred to as being **pinnately lobed** because the indentations of the margin do not extend as far as the midrib.

Ferns that have segmented or divided fronds, where the divisions are cut right to the midrib, are referred to as being **pinnate**. The primary divisions are known as **pinnae** (singular pinna). If the blade is just once-divided it is **simply pinnate** (refer to *Asplenium oblongifolium*); if the primary divisions are again divided it is said to be **twice pinnate** or **bi-pinnate** (refer to *Deparia petersenii*), and if the secondary divisions are again divided the blade is **three times pinnate** or **tri-pinnate** (refer to *Asplenium bulbiferum*). The fronds of some ferns may even be four-pinnate. The final divisions of a pinnate blade are known as **pinnules** (singular pinnule). They may have smooth or toothed margins.

Fern spores are produced in a small capsule known as a **sporangium** (plural sporangia). Sporangia usually occur on the more primitive species of ferns. The sporangia of most ferns are grouped together as a cluster, and a cluster of two or more sporangia is known as a **sorus** (plural sori). Sori have different shapes and in different species are found in different places: on the margin or underside of a lamina or front blade. The sporangia are protected by a membranous flap of tissue more or less covering

Main parts of a typical fern

Tufted rhizome.

Creeping rhizome.

Tree fern (caudex or trunk).

Simple frond.

Pinnately lobed frond.

Pinnate frond.

Twice pinnate frond.

Three-times pinnate frond.

Strobilus of a clubmoss.

Sori.

Sori.

Sori.

the sorus, known as an **indusium** (plural indusia). The diagrams on pages 8–9 illustrate the main parts of a typical fern. To enable readers to become familiar with the meanings of the terms used, a glossary is provided on pages 126–27.

With fern allies the sporangia may be solitary, in pairs or aggregated together into a fruiting body known as a **cone** or **strobilus** (plural strobili).

Distribution maps

The distribution maps, provided for each species, indicate the broader areas (in green shading) over which a species may be present. They are diagrammatic (not definitive) and do not necessarily imply that a particular species will occur in every part of the area indicated. Some species may have remarkably discontinuous distributions and, depending upon the part of the country, there may be considerable distances between the occurrence of a particular species.

New Zealand ferns and fern allies

Few countries are as well endowed with ferns as New Zealand. A generally mild climate and a usually abundant rainfall ensure that they numerically abound throughout most areas. While New Zealand is not as rich in species as some tropical countries, when it comes to general abundance it is a fern paradise. There are 194 species of native ferns and some 18 species of fern allies.

Naturally, the majority of species are found in forested areas, but some species also occur in various other habitats such as scrub, open country, wetlands, alpine areas and coastal areas.

The forests

New Zealand has two main kinds of forest: subtropical rainforest and subantarctic rainforest. Subtropical rainforest includes a mixture of coniferous trees (mainly belonging to the ancient Podocarpaceae family) and broad-leaved evergreens. Although the climate of present-day New Zealand is mainly warm-temperate, this forest is of distinctly subtropical origins. On the other hand the subantarctic rainforest (mainly *Nothofagus* or southern beech) is generally of a rather temperate nature. When exploring these forests the differences are quite obvious.

When entering New Zealand's rainforests, as well as looking for ferns on the ground it is also necessary to scan the tree trunks and even the mossy branches of the taller trees, because it will be observed that they grow in all available habitats. As might be expected, the subtropical rainforest is the richest: not only for the number of species but also for the sheer abundance of individuals.

The most noticeable group of native ferns is probably the tree ferns, of which there are six common species. In addition, there are two species that are somewhat anomalous, in that both may have stems that grow flat along the ground or, less commonly, have short, erect trunks. Tree ferns vary from the giant mamaku

(*Cyathea medullaris*), up to 20 m tall, to the more squat wheki-ponga (*Dicksonia fibrosa*), which is seldom more that 6 m tall. In disturbed forest or where the forest has been partially cleared, tree ferns usually regenerate rapidly, and the wheki (*Dicksonia squarrosa*) may often form conspicuous, dense thickets.

The humid conditions that generally prevail in the subtropical rainforests, particularly those of western regions, provide the ideal atmosphere for filmy ferns (*Hymenophyllum*) and their relatives, the bristle ferns (*Trichomanes*). With 21 species the genus *Hymenophyllum* contains the largest number of any fern genus in New Zealand. In most forested areas one or more species of them can generally be found. They are one of the most distinctive features of the fern vegetation and are so-named because of the usually delicate nature of their translucent fronds. They occur in considerable variety with some species growing on the ground or on rocks, while others may be found on tree trunks, tree fern trunks and the branches of trees. Filmy ferns vary from veritable giants with fronds from 40 cm long, or occasionally 60 cm, to quite diminutive species having fronds no more than 3 cm long.

Although their fronds are apparently very delicate, filmy ferns are surprisingly resilient to adverse conditions. In times of drought, or low humidity, their fronds will curl and shrivel so that they appear to be dead. However, some rain or dew will generally see them soon restored to their normal appearance.

Another usually easily identified group is that of the hard ferns (*Blechnum*). Several species may usually be found in most forest areas. Practically all *Blechnum* species have distinct fertile fronds that have a completely different appearance to what may be termed their normal or sterile fronds. During the growing season, the fertile fronds are usually green but have very narrow frond segments, so that they appear to almost belong to another species. With age they begin to darken and, when mature enough to shed their spores, usually turn brown and take on a shrivelled appearance. Along road and stream banks, and steep-sided gullies, the long, drooping fronds of the kiokio (*B. novae-zelandiae*) are a prominent feature in many forested areas. *Blechnum* is the second-largest group of native ferns.

The subantarctic rainforests generally contain fewer species and a lesser abundance of individuals, although they are very rich in mosses, liverworts and lichens. In the higher altitude forests the prickly shield-fern (*Polystichum vestitum*) is often common and forms magnificent clumps. One or two species of filmy fern (*Hymenophyllum*) may be quite common on the ground as well as on tree trunks. On the forest floor the alpine hard fern (*Blechnum penna-marina* subspecies *alpina*) may be observed creeping among the mosses, while the crown fern (*B. discolor*) often forms extensive colonies. In more open parts of the forest one of our few deciduous ferns (*Hypolepis millefolium*) forms spreading colonies. Occasional plants of the drooping spleenwort (*Asplenium flaccidum*) hang down from the mossy trunks of the beech trees (*Nothofagus*).

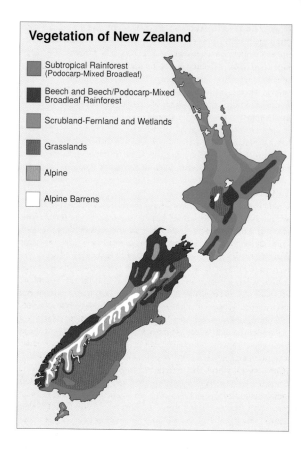

Vegetation of New Zealand

- Subtropical Rainforest (Podocarp-Mixed Broadleaf)
- Beech and Beech/Podocarp-Mixed Broadleaf Rainforest
- Scrubland-Fernland and Wetlands
- Grasslands
- Alpine
- Alpine Barrens

Clubmosses are not generally a feature of the forests and, apart from the drooping clubmoss (*Lycopodium varium*), those that do occur are mainly restricted to the better lit areas around the forest outskirts. *Lycopodium varium* usually grows perched on trees or rock faces. The fork fern (*Tmesipteris*) is seldom abundant, but it is easily recognised and it is nearly always possible to see it growing from tree fern trunks.

Scrublands

These are areas where multi-stemmed shrubs predominate. Depending upon the nature of the scrubland, the shrubs may be quite dense or inclined to be rather scattered. Sheltering under the scrub, it is often possible to find the necklace fern (*Asplenium flabellifolium*) and the ground spleenwort (*A. appendiculatum*). In more open scrublands, bracken (*Pteridium esculentum*) may be a common species. With the exception of eastern areas of both main islands, one of the two species of tangle fern (*Gleichenia*) may

12

often form a prominent part of some scrub associations. Quite often the prickly shield-fern becomes part of the scrubland and its presence often indicates that the area was once forested. Depending upon local climate, a not inconsiderable number of fern species may also occur in some scrublands. At least one of several species of clubmoss (*Lycopodium volubile*, *L. cernuum*, *L. deuterodensum*, *L. fastigiatum* and *L. scariosum*) may form a distinctive part of the scrubland vegetation.

Quite a number of scrubland areas are transitional, perhaps having once been forested and, if left undisturbed, will eventually return to forest. Depending upon local climatic conditions, this process may occur relatively quickly or may take many years.

Wetland habitats

Unlikely as it may seem, some ferns do occur in wetland habitats. Wetlands may occur around estuarine and coastal areas, lakes, rivers and poorly drained, low-lying ground. Within those various areas there may be ponds, swamps, bogs, and shrub and tree bogs. Each one will have its own distinct plant associations. Individual fern species may sometimes occur abundantly, but there is not usually a great variety of species. Some inhabitants of wetland areas are not necessarily wetland plants, but rather opportunists that take advantage of suitable habitats within the wetland itself.

If the ground is just marshy, the alpine hard fern (*Blechnum penna-marina* subspecies *alpina*) can be found creeping through the turfy vegetation, while the swamp kiokio (*B. minus*) will grow around pond margins or on the trunk-like bases of the large sedge (*Carex secta*), where they rise above the water. In western areas, particularly on pakihi country (poorly drained, open or barren land; see glossary), one or more species of tangle fern (*Gleichenia*) may also occur in boggy ground. A search may also reveal the tiny comb fern (*Schizaea australis*) growing among open places in scrub. If there are suitable ponds or small lakes the green or reddish mats of the floating water fern (*Azolla filiculoides*) often occur, but drainage of wetland areas has destroyed much of its habitat.

Grasslands and open country

The ubiquitous bracken (*Pteridium esculentum*) frequently occurs in grasslands but on the drier country it seldom grows very tall. The alpine hard fern (*Blechnum penna-marina* subspecies *alpina*) may also be a common component of such vegetation. Ferns are not necessarily confined to moist places, and in rocky areas one of the species of *Pellaea* may occur. Some of these ferns are quite anomalous, generally being collectively known as 'hot-rock ferns' because they usually inhabit dry, sunny situations on rock faces and bluffs. The two species of *Cheilanthes* are the ones most likely to be seen. During times of stress their fronds will curl and shrivel so that they appear to be dead, but a shower of rain revives them to show that they are still alive and healthy. Another species that usually grows in sunny locations, mostly on limestone rock, is the maidenhair spleenwort (*Asplenium trichomanes*).

Whangarei
Auckland
NORTH ISLAND
Hamilton
Rotorua
Gisborne
New Plymouth
Napier
Palmerston North
Nelson
Wellington
Greymouth
SOUTH ISLAND
Christchurch
Timaru
Dunedin
Invercargill
STEWART ISLAND

Alpine areas

Several ferns occur in the subalpine and alpine vegetation of mountain areas. It may appear strange to find a filmy fern in such an extreme environment, but *Hymenophyllum multifidum* not infrequently occurs in subalpine scrub. Often it appears to resemble a curled-up patch of moss, but once its fronds have been moistened by dew or rain it soon shows that it is truly a filmy fern. One tiny fern that is easily overlooked is *Grammitis poeppigiana*. It has spoon-shaped fronds no more than 3 cm long and forms small, mossy patches on rocks. The ubiquitous alpine hard fern also occurs in many alpine regions. The mountain kiokio is another species that occurs in subalpine scrub/grassland or on rocky areas. One or two species of clubmoss are not uncommon. Species most likely to be observed are the alpine clubmoss (*Lycopodium fastigiatum*) and the creeping clubmoss (*L. scariosum*).

Coastal areas

In the comparative shelter of coastal forests and scrub quite a number of ferns may occur, but there are two species of hard fern (*Blechnum*) that will actually grow close to the high-water mark. They are frequently splashed with salt water but show no ill effects from it. *Blechnum durum* is restricted to the coast around the southern part of the South Island, while *B. blechnoides* has a wider distribution from North Cape southwards. This latter species is never found far from the influence of salt spray. Three species of spleenwort (*Asplenium*) may also grow in exposed places but are

14

generally happier in more sheltered situations. They are the shining spleenwort (*A. oblongifolium*) and *A. scleroprium*. On mainland New Zealand, the latter occurs only around the southern coastline of the South Island. The shore spleenwort (*A. obtusatum*) will endure more exposed habitats and can be found on coastal rocks where it is subject to salt spray.

Using the key to identify the ferns

There are 26 letters, or steps, to the key, each giving two choices or answers. The key is based entirely on frond (leaf) growth and habit and, to lesser degree, on sorus (spore case) characters.

To begin

Always commence at **A**. Decide whether your plant is a floating aquatic or growing on or in the ground, on trees or on rocks. Having done that, proceed to whichever step is next indicated (letters in the column on the right-hand side of the page). Continue through the key until you arrive at a number or group of numbers, in **bold type**, which will then refer you to suggested text page numbers. You can then compare your plant with the text and photographs until you find one that matches. Not all ferns and fern allies are in the guide, so that if you have come across a less common species it may not be possible to identify it.

Example

Beginning at **A**. If the plant that you wish to identify is a small aquatic plant floating on the surface of a pond, you should go directly to the **text and photograph on p. 125**. If it grows in or on the ground, on trees or on rocks, you are then referred to step **B**. This step gives you a choice of *'Plants tree-like, usually with a single trunk'*, or *'Plants not as above, not usually having distinct trunks'*. If the plant you are trying to identify is tall and tree-like and grows on a single trunk, you are then referred to **pp. 69–77, 114, 118**. This takes you to the tree ferns or ferns with trunks. If you then refer to those entries it should not be too difficult to match your plant with one of the species illustrated.

The second choice for step **B** states: *'Plants not as above, not usually having distinct trunks …C'*. Should that be the case, it is then necessary to go to step **C**. From there on, by a simple, continuing process of elimination, you should eventually be able to match your plant with the appropriate text and illustration. The distribution maps with each entry will also help.

Range of use

This key is designed for use on adult ferns, and fern allies, and is not intended for use on juvenile forms or immature plants. It is meant to be only an aid to identification and is not intended to be 100 per cent accurate. For example, older plants of some ferns may rise up on short trunks but they are not generally considered to be tree ferns.

Key to the species described

A. Small aquatic plant floating on pond surfaces ....**p. 125**
    Plants growing on or in ground, on trees or on rocks ....**B**

B. Tree-like, usually with a single trunk ......**pp. 69–77, 114, 118**
    Plants not as above, not usually having distinct trunks ....**C**

C. Vine-like plant, only north of Kawhia, Bay of Plenty ......**p. 30**
    Plants tufted or creeping on/in ground, on trees/rocks.........**D**

D. Plants moss-like, not at all fern-like.....................................**X**
    Plants fern-like and not having a moss-like appearance ......**E**

E. Ferns with fertile fronds that usually appear like shrivelled
    versions of the normal or sterile fronds...............**pp. 111–123**
    Ferns not as above...**F**

F. Fronds having a translucent or see-through nature.............**W**
    Fronds not as above, usually opaque ....**G**

G. Primary frond segments in flattened pairs at top of stem, or
    repeatedly forking in whorls to form tangled thicket............**Z**
    Primary frond segments not as above................................**H**

H. Spore cases scattered over undersurfaces of fronds...............**I**
    Spore cases usually as clustered capsules at tips of bare
    stalks, or on upper surfaces of special fertile leaves.............**V**

I. Spore cases under margins of frond segments, as continuous
    lines, or as individual capsules, sometimes projecting
    from margins......................................**pp. 33–44, 79, 87–88**
    Spore cases not as above...**J**

J. Fronds simple, strap-shaped, not lobed or divided..**pp. 50–54**
    Fronds not as above ....**K**

K. Fronds lobed..**pp. 52–53, 109, 113**
    Fronds once or much divided ....**L**

L. Fronds once-divided...**M**
    Fronds divided more than once ....**N**

M. Frond divisions usually less than 4 cm long, longer on some
    species, margins smooth or toothed.....................**pp. 40, 49,**
    85–86, 90, 96, 99, 109–111, 114–115, 117, 120, 122–123
    Divisions usually more than 4 cm long, shorter on small
    plants ....**pp. 94–96, 97–98, 109, 113, 119, 121, 123**

N. Plants with tufted bases, not forming patches or colonies....**O**
    Plants with creeping roots, forming patches or colonies.......**U**

O. Fronds may be large, to 1.5 m or longer ....**pp. 27, 69, 101**
    Fronds usually shorter...**P**

P. Frond divisions simple, quite narrow and toothed..........**p. 49**
    Frond divisions not as above ....**Q**

Q. Frond stalks scaly or hairy ....**pp. 77, 89, 91, 92–94, 98, 103**
    Frond stalks not as above...**R**

R. Fronds triangular and distinctly widest at bases ..**pp. 102–105**
    Fronds triangular but narrower, bases not wider ....**S**

S. Fronds harsh to touch, stalks and midribs scaly ..**pp. 106–107**
    Fronds not as above ....**T**

T. Fronds broadly triangular ....**pp. 69, 75, 78, 102, 105**
    Fronds narrower, triangular or not triangular......................**V**

U. Larger ferns, principal segments of fronds once or
    twice divided...**pp. 93, 100, 104, 108**
    Medium to smaller ferns, principal segments of fronds three-
    to four-times divided............**pp. 78, 81–84, 93, 100, 104, 108**

V. Fronds not present, stalks stiff and wiry with tight clusters of
    spore cases at their tips...**pp. 31–32**
    Plants not as above, usually growing from tree fern trunk,
    sterile leaves on either side of drooping stems, spore cases
    either single or paired on upper surfaces of fertile leaves ..**p. 18**

W. Fronds mostly less than 40 cm long, translucent.....**pp. 55–68**
    Plants much larger, fronds usually more than 50 cm long, of
    a translucent or see-through nature.......................**pp. 28–29**

X. Plants moss-like, tufted, in ground or on trees........**pp. 19, 25**
    Plants moss-like but not as above ....**Y**

Y. Plants creeping over ground, forming patches or colonies,
    usually less than 50 cm tall....................................**pp. 22–24**
    Plants taller, erect, or scrambling ....**pp. 20, 21, 26**

Z. Fronds umbrella-shaped......................................**pp. 47–48**
    Fronds repeatedly forked, in tangled thickets ....**pp. 45–46, 18**

In spite of their common name these are not true ferns at all, but belong to a small group of very primitive spore-producing plants having a longer fossil record than the ferns, and they also have no close relatives. As well as in New Zealand, the genus occurs in Australia, Tasmania and the Pacific Islands. There are four native species and they are distinguished mainly by the sporangia (spore-producing capsules) that are produced on the upper surfaces of the fertile leaves. Interestingly, the fork ferns have creeping, branched underground stems but do not have actual roots. Aerial **stems** are usually pendulous or drooping and varying from about 10–80 cm in length. **Leaves** (actually lobes that are leaf-like) are spirally arranged around the stem or arranged along either side, 1–3 cm long, narrowly ovate to oblong, usually with shortly pointed tips. The forked **fertile leaves** each bear, on their upper surfaces, a pair of **spore cases** in the angle of the fork. Superficially, the four species of fork ferns are all very similar, and it is the size and shape of their spore cases that helps to identify them. Two of the species have rather restricted distributions in coastal and lowland forests, in both the North and South Islands, while *T. elongata* and *T. tannensis* are more widely distributed in lowland to montane forests in both main islands. In addition they occur on Stewart and the Chatham Islands, with the latter species extending down to the subantarctic islands. Fork ferns most commonly grow as epiphytes on tree fern trunks, occasionally on rocks or, particularly on Stewart Island, from among the mounded debris at the bases of forest trees. (*T. elongata* is illustrated.)

Tufted clubmoss *Lycopodium australianum*

Unlike most other native species of club-moss the tufted clubmoss grows as a smallish clump and does not have creeping rhizomes or stems. Depending upon habitat it varies from 5–20 cm tall. It will attain about 30 cm tall under favourable conditions. Its stems are rigid, erect and forking or branching several times into stout and rigid branches. It is densely leafy with the **sterile leaves** being spirally arranged around the stem. They are lance-shaped with sharp, almost pungent points, and up to 1 cm long. The **fertile leaves** are clustered near the tips of the stems. They are similar to the sterile leaves and have solitary **sporangia** in their axils. The tufted clubmoss is found in the North, South and Stewart Islands and also extends down to the subantarctic islands. It is common in mountain regions from the Raukumara Range and Rotorua southwards. It often grows in rocky places in snow tussock grasslands, herbfields, and in subalpine scrub, particularly in the higher rainfall regions. In the far south it comes down to lower altitudes, particularly on Stewart Island. The species ranges from 600–1700 m. It also occurs in Australia and Borneo, and is sometimes known as *Huperzia australiana*.

LYCOPODIACEAE

This species of club-moss is very distinct, and easily recognised, and it is strange that it does not appear to have any common name. Its main **stems** may be up to 5 m long and loop across the ground, rooting in at intervals. The **aerial stems** arise from between the rooting points and, to the casual observer, resemble seedlings of that tall forest tree, the rimu (*Dacrydium cupressinum*). On large plants they are erect and may be up to 1 m tall, but are usually less. They are much-branched with the **branchlets** curving downwards at their

tips. The **sterile leaves** are crowded, about 5 mm long, needle-like and arranged spirally around the stem. The **strobili** or spore cones form at the tips of the drooping branchlets and are up to 1.5 cm long. *Lycopodium cernuum* occurs in lowland to lower montane regions of the North Island from near North Cape to Lake Taupo, and in the South Island from north-western Nelson and the Marlborough Sounds southwards down the western side to Okarito. It usually grows on open roadsides and banks, under light scrub on moorland and in boggy country. It is particularly abundant in the heated ground near the thermal springs of the North Island. This species is sometimes listed as *Lycopodiella cernuua*.

Strobili.

Puakarimu *Lycopodium deuterodensum*

Lycopodium deuterodensum is another most striking and distinct species of clubmoss, which like *L. cernuum* (previous page) resembles a small coniferous tree. It often forms quite extensive colonies but, sometimes, depending upon surrounding shrub growth, its stems may be more scattered. Its much-branched aerial **stems** are erect and generally 60 cm to 1 m tall. The **sterile leaves** vary from 1–3 mm long and are of three forms, ranging from densely pressed all around the branchlet to being spreading and occurring side by side. Individual branchlets will generally bear one form only. They are spirally arranged around the branchlet. The **strobili** are up to 3 cm long and erect from the tips of the branchlets. Generally, the puakarimu has a more slender appearance than *L. cernuum* and is usually less symmetrical. It is common, in the North Island, from North Cape to Lake Taupo, occurring mainly around forest margins, in scrub or in regenerating kauri forest. It also occurs on the Chatham Islands.

Alpine clubmoss *Lycopodium fastigiatum*

This is one of the commonest species of clubmoss, particularly at higher altitudes, and it occurs in mountain districts throughout the North, South, Stewart and Chatham Islands. The alpine clubmoss also ranges far to the south, occurring on the subantarctic islands. Its underground **rhizomes** are stout and branching. The aerial **stems** are rigid and erect and may be up to 40 cm tall, although generally

shorter. Their upper portions are densely branched. The **sterile leaves** are 3–5 mm long, spirally arranged and closely overlapping with their tips curving inwards. Generally, they are green, but in exposed situations they may be quite orange. The yellowish **cones** or **strobili** are up to 7 cm long and erect on rather long stalks. They are either solitary or in groups of two to three. In size this is a variable plant and is often much reduced in exposed habitats. In the North Island it occurs from the Coromandel Peninsula southwards. The species usually grows in subalpine scrub, alpine

herbfields, grasslands and bogs. It is found from 200–2000 m. In the southern part of its range it descends into lowland areas. Usually, it is easily recognised by its erect cones, incurved leaves and frequently by the orange colour that it often assumes.

Strobili.

Bog clubmoss *Lycopodium laterale*

Bog clubmoss is a distinct species that is not easily mistaken for any other clubmoss (apart from *L. diffusum*, which differs in being shorter with prostrate stems and is not described here). Its **rhizome** is much-branched and its **aerial stems** are up to 30 cm tall, erect and rigid or sometimes rather weak, not branched but sometimes may have a few branches. The **sterile leaves** are spirally arranged, erect to spreading, up to 7 mm long, narrow and sharply pointed, dull green and sometimes with a reddish brown tinge. The solitary **fertile cones** or **strobili** are erect, not stalked, up to 3 cm long, produced from the side of the main stem, or terminal on short branchlets, and are dark chocolate-brown at maturity. Bog clubmoss occurs in the North Island from North Cape to the Waikato, and very localised in the southern part of the island. In the South Island it is found from north-western Nelson to northern Westland. It also occurs on the Chatham Islands. Generally, it grows in lowland to montane boggy areas and moorlands. This species is also known as *Lycopodiella lateralis*.

LYCOPODIACEAE

The creeping clubmoss is quite distinct and is usually easily recognised by its flattened leaves and solitary, stalked cones. It has rather stout, creeping main **stems** that are branched and up to 2 m long. The aerial stems are freely branched and may be up to 50 cm tall, but are quite often shorter. The **sterile leaves** are up to 4 mm long and are flattened in the one plane. A close examination of the stem will show that the leaves are

of two sizes: the large ones that spread out from either side of the stem and smaller ones that lie flattened along the stem, between the larger ones. The **cones** are erect on unbranched stalks and are 2.5–5 cm long. When young they are pale yellowish and then with age turn brownish. The creeping clubmoss is found throughout the North, South, Stewart and Chatham Islands, and also extends down to the subantarctic islands. Although rare in Northland, it is fairly common throughout the rest of the country except for the dry, east-coast areas of both main islands. It often forms thick, spreading patches on banks and in scrub in montane and subalpine areas. Especially in scrub country it may behave as a semi-climber, scrambling up through the stems of adjoining shrubs for quite a height.

Drooping clubmoss *Lycopodium varium*

This species comprises two distinct forms: one that is epiphytic on forest trees and the other a smaller, erect, terrestrial form that grows in rocky ground or in scrub and open forest. The epiphytic form is a most handsome clubmoss, particularly when it grows as a large plant. It occurs in lowland and montane forests as an epiphyte on trees or, less commonly, on rock faces and is the only epiphytic clubmoss in New Zealand. It hangs down in long tassels with the **stems** forking numerous times. On particularly large specimens the stems may be as long as 2 m, although usually up to about 1.5 m would be a good length. The **sterile leaves** are arranged in spiral fashion, up to 2 cm long and decreasing in size towards the tips of the stems. The slender, pendulous **strobili** are distinctly four-angled, occasionally forked, and the **fertile leaves** are often barely distinct from the sterile ones. Although both forms usually grow in different habitats there is no doubt that they belong to the one species. *Lycopodium varium* occurs on the Kermadec and Three Kings Islands, and is quite widespread in the North, South and Stewart Islands, on the Chatham Islands and down to the subantarctic islands. It also occurs in Australia. The species is variously known as hanging clubmoss, tassel fern and iwitu-na. It is sometimes listed as *Huperzia varia*.

Scrambling clubmoss *Lycopodium volubile*

The scrambling clubmoss is distinct and easily recognised. It has long main **stems** that scramble through undergrowth or sprawl over the ground and may be up to 5 m in length. As with *L. scariosum* its **sterile leaves** are flattened into the one plane with two sizes of leaves. The larger leaves are about 5 mm long and spread out from each side of the stem, while the smaller leaves lie flattened along the stem between the larger ones. The **strobili** are about 8 cm long and are pendulous, in large clusters, on much-branched stalks. When ripe they are a pale yellow turning yellow-brown with age and are usually a conspicuous feature on the plant. It is common in lowland and montane scrublands and forest margins, occurring on the Kermadec and Three Kings Islands and then throughout the North, South and Stewart Islands and on the Chatham Islands. The species is not very common along the dry eastern side of the South Island. It also occurs in south-eastern Asia, New Guinea, New Caledonia and Australia. *Lycopodium volubile* is also known as the climbing clubmoss, owl's foot and waewaekoukou. It was once popular with florists for use in wreaths and floral arrangements. In former times its long stems were much used for decorating country dance halls.

Strobili.

King fern *Marattia salicina*

Apart from the tree ferns this is one of the most magnificent of our native ferns. It is a terrestrial fern that has a large, irregularly shaped, tuber-like **rootstock** and, when well grown, has thick, heavy fronds that may be up to 4 m long by up to 1.5 m broad. Its rootstock is actually formed from the long-persisting, fleshy bases of the fronds. The **stipes** (frond stalks) are thick and fleshy and up to 1 m in length. Its frond **blades** are 3–4 m by 0.6–1.5 m and are a deep, glossy green. They are twice-pinnate with the **secondary pinnae** being oblong, 5–20 cm by 1–2.5 cm, pointed at their apexes and rounded at their bases. The boat-shaped **sori** are grouped around the margins on the undersides of the **pinnules**. The king fern used to be common in lowland forests of the North Island, from Kaitaia to the Bay of Plenty and southern Taranaki, but because of the depredations of wild pigs, and other browsing stock, it is now rather uncommon. It usually grows in dark gullies in heavy bush, and scattered populations of it still occur in the Auckland, Waikato, Coromandel and northern Taranaki regions. In pre-European times the large, starchy rootstock was an important source of food for Maori, who also cultivated it near their villages. *Marattia salicina* is also known as para and horseshoe fern. The latter name derives from the basal portion of the frond that adheres to the rootstock, which is shaped like a horse's hoof.

Crepe fern *Leptopteris hymenophylloides*

A lovely and delicate, dark-green fern that lives in moist forests, crepe fern can be recognised by the translucent nature of its finely cut fronds. It grows to about 60 cm tall. Usually, it grows on a short **trunk** 20–40 cm tall, sometimes more, and clad with the bases of the old frond stalks. The **stipes** are 15–50 cm long, slender, and olive green to pale brown. The **frond blade** is narrowly triangular, 50 cm to 1m long by 15–35 cm broad, three-times pinnate with the main pinnae in 20 to 30 pairs. The final divisions of the frond blade are very finely cut. The brown **sporangia** are scattered over the undersurface of the frond and are not clustered into distinct sori. The soft, feathery fronds, together with the fact that it often grows up on a short trunk, will help to identify this fern. If any other confirmation is needed it is only necessary to hold it up to the light so that its translucency can be seen. The crepe fern is common in lowland and montane forests throughout the North, South and Stewart Islands, as well as on the Chatham Islands. It is especially common in damp gullies. *Leptopteris hymenophylloides* is also known as heruheru and single crepe fern.

28

Prince of Wales feathers *Leptopteris superba*

This is surely the most beautiful of our native ferns, and is found in cool, wet forests. It grows on a **rootstock** that may be up to 1 m tall but is usually less. The rootstock is surrounded by a mass of fibrous roots so that it usually assumes a distinctive, more or less conical appearance. The fronds are quite wide-spreading on **stipes** up to 8 cm long. The **frond blade** is from 40 cm to 1.2 m long by 10–20 cm broad and tapering to both its base and apex. It is three-times pinnate and the 35 to 60 pairs of **primary pinnae** are crowded. The **ultimate segments** are very narrow and stand up at an angle of about 90 degrees so as to give the frond a double or crested appearance. This, combined with the deep green and translucent nature of its fronds, gives it a most beautiful appearance. The Prince of Wales feathers occurs throughout the North, South and Stewart Islands in montane forests. It is rare in Northland, but is common from the Bay of Plenty to Wellington. In the South Island it is abundant down the western side of the island, but is rare on the east. It is also known as double crepe fern, ngutungutu kiwi, ngutukakariki and heruheru.

Mangemange *Lygodium articulatum*

Mangemange is one of the most unusual ferns in New Zealand. It climbs and scrambles over shrubs and small trees and even up to the tops of tall forest trees. What appear to be its woody, climbing stems are actually the **midribs** of the **fronds**, and so it has the longest fronds of any native fern. Instead of stopping, as most ferns do, its fronds continue to grow indefinitely and may, ultimately, be up to 30 m or more in length. Mangemange is further distinguished by having separate **sterile** and **fertile pinnae** on the one frond. The primary **pinnae** branch in twos and the oval final segments are 4–10 cm long by 0.5–2 cm broad. Their upper surfaces are usually bright green and the undersurfaces blue-green. The **fertile pinnae** are branched or forked numerous times and end in fan-shaped, lobed segments 0.5–1 cm long. The species is confined to the upper half of the North Island from North Cape to Kawhia and the Bay of Plenty. It is abundant in lowland forests and may sometimes form dense and impenetrable tangles. *Lygodium* is also known as makamaka and bushman's mattress. The latter name derives from the use to which the tangled, wiry stems were sometimes put. The stems, or midribs, were used for making ropes and twine by old-time Maori.

Southern comb fern *Shizaea australis*

As well as being primitive, the comb ferns are unusual in that they do not have fronds in the more generally accepted sense of the term. Usually, they are also inconspicuous, growing in small tufts or clumps of what appear to be wiry, leafless stalks or **stipes**. The stipes are from 2.5–15 cm long and generally are seldom completely straight and often have slight bends, particularly towards their upper halves. The **'sterile fronds'** have no visible blades and it is only the **fertile frond** that has a comb-like cluster of four to eight fertile segments, or pinnae, standing erect from its tip. What may be termed the **blade** of the fertile frond is from 0.5–1.5 cm long. The southern comb fern grows in poor and barren soils in short grassland of boggy ground, or turfy vegetation. It occurs through the North, South, Stewart, Auckland and Campbell Islands. It is often local in subalpine areas of mountain districts and in the North Island it is found from Mount Moehau southwards. In the South Island it is mainly found west of the main divide but, in the far south,

descends to sea level. It is not easily seen and a diligent search in likely localities might need to be made before it can be located.

Fan fern *Schizaea dichotoma*

This species of comb fern is most distinctive because the upper portions of its **stipes** are branched or forked four to 10 times, or more, so that they have a fan-shaped appearance. This unmistakable fern is quite uncommon and easily overlooked. It is confined to the upper half of the North Island, from Kaitaia and Mangonui to Kawhia and Tauranga, where it mainly grows in lowland kauri forests. It also occurs in the heated soils of thermal areas between Rotorua and Taupo. In addition it is found on the Kermadec Islands and Mayor Island. The fan fern grows from 10–30 cm tall with the **branches** of the stipes being up to 10 cm long and with a spread of 5–10 cm. The **fertile blades** occur as tiny tufts of segments, at the tips of each branch, and are from 3–5 mm long. The **sporangia** are in two closely placed rows. As well as occurring in New Zealand, it also occurs in tropical and subtropical regions of both hemispheres from Madagascar to the Pacific.

True maidenhair *Adiantum aethiopicum*

Of all the native species of maidenhair ferns this one is most easily recognised because it more closely resembles the exotic maiden-hair ferns that are commonly grown as indoor plants. It has creeping **rhizomes**, with tufts of fronds at intervals, and will form quite large colonies, often to the exclusion of almost all other small plants. The slender **stipes** are 5–25 cm long, dark brown to almost black, and shiny. The **frond blades** are 10–30 cm long by 6–15 cm broad and in their basal portions are two- to three-times pinnate. The **ultimate segments** are fan-shaped on rather slender stalks. Being the only New Zealand species with fan-shaped ultimate segments makes the species readily recognisable. The **sporangia** are placed in the notches of the margins of each segment and are protected by rather large kidney-shaped **indusia**. The whole frond is pale green and has a very delicate appearance. *Adiantum aethiopicum* occurs in lowland forests and scrub of the North Island from North Cape to Waikato and is then rather local from there to the Wairarapa area. The fern is also quite widely distributed in tropical and subtropical countries. This species is also known as makaka.

Common maidenhair *Adiantum cunninghamii*

This is the commonest and most widely distributed of the native maidenhair ferns and it occurs throughout most of New Zealand except for dry eastern areas. It may be recognised by its creeping habit and the fact that its fronds are completely devoid of hairs. It is further distinguished by the fronds often being much-branched, although when growing in more exposed situations they may be barely branched and often reduced to just a few centimetres in length. The ultimate segments of the frond are quite large and oblong. The **rhizomes** are rather wide-spreading. The **stipes** are 8–25 cm long, almost black, shiny and hairless. The blade of the **frond** is 15–30 cm long by 7–20 cm wide, with the basal portion two-to three-times pinnate and then simply pinnate above. **Ultimate segments** (pinnae) are more or less oblong, with the upper margin irregularly toothed. Upper surfaces are deep green, and blue-green beneath. **Sporangia** occur in small notches around the upper margins and are protected by kidney-shaped **indusia**. *Adiantum cunninghamii* is distributed from the Kermadec and Three Kings Islands, through the North, South and Stewart Islands, thence eastwards to the Chatham Islands. It is generally common in coastal and lowland forests, forest remnants, and on cliffs and banks. The species is often found in drier forests rather than wet ones. Although not confined to limestone areas, it may be fairly common on limestone rocks. The fern seldom occurs at high elevations. It is sometimes known as the blue maidenhair.

Small maidenhair *Adiantum diaphanum*

This is the smallest of the native species of maidenhair ferns. It is easily recognised because its fronds are either unbranched or have just one pair of main branches (rarely two pairs). The blade of the frond is a pale green and often simply pinnate. The **rhizome** is short and erect and the very slender, dark brown **stipes** are 5–15 cm long. The blade of the **frond** is 5–10 cm long by 1.5–3 cm wide and has a rather delicate appearance (in fact the name 'diaphanum' means semi-transparent). The **ultimate segments** are more or less oblong, 15 x 8 mm and are on very slender stalks. There are usually four to eight **sporangia** per segment placed in the small notches along the upper and outer margins, and the **indusia** are characteristically kidney-shaped. *Adiantum diaphanum* ranges throughout the North Island and in the South Island to about the Marlborough Sounds and Nelson. It also occurs on the Kermadec Islands. Generally, it occurs mainly in coastal and lowland forests, quite often on dry, shaded banks, under rock overhangs or along rocky stream margins. As well as occurring in New Zealand the small maidenhair is also found in Norfolk Island, Australia and from Fiji to southern China.

Giant maidenhair *Adiantum formosum*

The giant maidenhair is the largest of New Zealand's maidenhair ferns and it also has the most restricted distribution of any native species. A handsome fern, it may be recognised by its very large and much-branched fronds. It has a widely creeping **rhizome** and will form quite a large colony. The black and shiny **stipes** may be up to 70 cm tall and are rough to the touch. The dark green **frond blade** is 28–80 cm long by 20–50 cm wide and is three- to four-times pinnate. The **ultimate segments** are more or less oblong and are regularly lobed around their upper margins; the segments are up to 15 x 5 mm. The **sporangia** are situated around the upper margins of the segments and protected by crescent-shaped **indusia**. The giant maidenhair was formerly found in one or two Northland localities, including Herekino and the Northern Wairoa River, but is now confined to the southern North Island in the Manawatu Gorge area. It occurs in lowland forest areas in deep alluvial soils. Although rare in New Zealand the fern is common in Australia. It is also known as the plumed maidenhair.

Adiantum fulvum

This species can be confused with the common maidenhair but can always be identified by its stipes being rough to the touch and the midribs of the frond being hairy. It has a creeping **rhizome** and forms small to largish colonies. Its **stipes** are 10–30 cm long and roughened. The **frond blades** are 15–35 cm long by 10–25 cm wide, more symmetrical and usually a darker green than *A. cunninghamii*, and they are two- to three-times pinnate. The **ultimate segments** are generally narrower and more pointed than those of *A. cunninghamii* as well as having dark green to pale green undersurfaces. The **sporangia** are in shallow notches at the tips of the segment lobes and are protected by kidney-shaped **indusia**. It grows in the North and South Islands, being common from North Cape to Taranaki and the Bay of Plenty, but is then more localised southwards to Banks Peninsula. Usually, it can be found in coastal forest around margins, in more open forest and on banks. Although it may be sometimes confused with *A. cunninghamii* it is never as common. The species is endemic.

PTERIDACEAE

Rosy maidenhair may be recognised by its distinctively forked fronds that have a rather stiff and harsh texture and a broadly fan-shaped outline. It has a stout and shortly creeping **rhizome** with the fronds tufted. The dark brown to almost black **stipes** are 15–30 cm long and rough to the touch. The **frond blade** is 12–30 cm long by 10–25 cm in width and is usually a deep olive green with the young fronds often being reddish. It is branched at the base with each branch usually again being forked so that ultimately there may be up to 10 branches. The **ultimate segments** are more or less oblong with finely toothed upper margins. The **sporangia** are situated in small notches around the upper and outer margins, and are protected with kidney-shaped **indusia**. In the North Island the rosy maidenhair is common from North Cape to Raglan and the Bay of Plenty, and then with scattered populations southwards to Levin. It also occurs on the Kermadec and Three Kings Islands, as well as on the Chatham Islands. It has been recorded from one or two South Island localities but is most likely extinct there. The fern can usually be found on dry, sunny banks, in rocky places and in open forests and coastal forest. It is sometimes referred to as the bristly maidenhair.

Woolly-cloak fern *Cheilanthes distans*

Woolly-cloak fern is one of a small group of ferns that shun the typical moist and shady fern habitats and instead prefer to grow in dry, sunny situations. Apart from the fact that it grows in dry and sunny situations, characters that help to identify it are the young fronds being hairy as they unfurl and the sori being almost continuous around the margins of the frond segments. The **fronds** are tufted at the top of a short **rhizome**, the stiff, wiry **stipes** are from 2–12 cm in length and are a dark chestnut brown. The dark green **frond blade** is pinnate to twice-pinnate, very narrow in outline and 3–15 cm long by 1–3 cm wide. Its **ultimate segments** are broad and variously cut and lobed around their margins. As the fronds unfurl their young parts are conspicuously clad with white

hairs. The **sori** are almost continuous around the margins, which are just slightly rolled to give them a little protection. The woolly-cloak fern occurs through both the North and South Islands, in coastal to montane areas from the Bay of Islands to Banks Peninsula. It does not occur in western areas, being a plant of the drier eastern side of the country. Generally, it grows in dry, rocky places and normally in full sun. In drought conditions its fronds will shrivel and appear to be dead, only to revive after being wetted by rain. Woolly-cloak fern also occurs in Australia and New Caledonia. It is also known as the woolly rock fern or blanket fern. *Cheilanthes sieberi* is a similar species that is distinguished by the crooks of the young fronds not being hairy or woolly.

Hot rock pellaea *Pellaea calidirupium*

Until relatively recently, this fern was recognised as a distinct species, although it was not named. It has since been named as a distinct species and is quite common in various areas of the country. It is another fern that prefers to grow in dry and sunny situations. It has a creeping and slowly spreading **rhizome** that may form small to largish colonies. The fronds are usually numerous and clustered along the rhizome. Its dark brown **stipes** are 3–25 cm long. The rather narrow **frond blade** is 3–30 cm long by 1.5–5.5 cm wide and is simply pinnate. The **pinnae** are 8–40 mm long by 4–15 mm wide. On very small plants they may be reduced to just one largish terminal pinna, or a terminal pinna with just one pair of lateral pinnae. Generally the **sori** are continuous around the margins of the fertile pinnae. *Pellaea calidirupium* is distributed in both the North and South Islands from the east coast of Northland southwards to Cook Strait and then down the eastern side of the South Island to Central Otago. It usually occurs in dry and open rocky locations of coastal to montane areas. It may have a rather discontinuous distribution. In Central Otago it is not uncommon and may often be abundant on rock ledges and in crevices. In the more sheltered situations it attains its maximum size, but in exposed places plants may be quite diminutive. Hot rock pellaea also occurs in Australia.

Pellaea falcata

This is a handsome fern, having dark green fronds of which the pinnae are commonly referred to as being sickle-shaped but, in reality, they are not strongly curved and hooked, and are actually scythe-shaped. It has a shortly creeping **rhizome** and its dark brown, erect **stipes** are 7–25 cm long. The long and narrow **frond blade** is 20–50 cm long by 3–7 cm wide, with regularly spaced pinnae. Its oblong **pinnae** are 1.5–4 cm long by 7–15 mm wide and taper to a sharp

point. They are either straight or slightly curved, upper surfaces shiny, undersurfaces paler. The **sori** run around each margin but do not join together at the apex. It is found on the Kermadec and Three Kings Islands, while in the North Island it is confined to coastal areas north of Auckland. Usually, it can be found in small patches growing on open banks, under light bush, or in pohutukawa forest. This species is closely allied to the next fern (*P. rotundifolia*) which, in some of its forms, can be confused with *P. falcata*. There are forms of *P. rotundifolia* that have quite long pinnae not dissimilar to those of *P. falcata*. It is not yet known whether they are simply clonal forms of *P. rotundifolia* or possibly a distinct species.

Button fern *Pellaea rotundifolia*

The button fern is an attractive species that is recognised by its usually rounded dark green pinnae set along a dark brown, bristly midrib. Sometimes, forms are encountered that have longer and more sharply pointed pinnae and appear to resemble *P. falcata*. Such plants are more common along the eastern coast of the North Island, the Wellington region, north-west Nelson and the Marlborough Sounds. The button fern has a creeping **rhizome** and may form quite large colonies. Its **stipes** are 5–20 cm long, very dark brown and bristly. The **frond blade** is long and narrow, 15–40 cm long by 1.8–4 cm wide. It is simply pinnate and the **pinnae** are 8–20 mm by 5–13 mm with either rounded tips or with short, sharp points. The **sori** run around the margins of the pinnae but do not join at their tips. The button fern occurs on the Three Kings Islands and in lowland to montane forests, throughout the North and South Islands as far south as Invercargill, but is rare on the west coast of the South Island. It is also on the Chatham Islands. It ranges from sea level to 600 m. While it often favours dry, rocky places in forest or light scrub it also occurs in some rainforests. Not infrequently it will grow in rocky places in the open. The button fern is also known as the round-leaved fern and tarawera.

Sweet fern *Pteris macilenta*

This is a beautiful fern that may be recognised by its fronds having a more open appearance than other species of *Pteris*, the attrractive, pale green colour of its fronds and the segments often being stalked. *Pteris macilenta* is found in the North, South and Chatham Islands, usually in drier and more open forests. Except for central regions it is common in the North Island but in the South Island is mainly confined to Nelson and west of the main divide. It extends south to northern Fiordland but is uncommon south of Greymouth. It has a short and erect **rhizome**. Its yellowish or brownish **stipes** are 10–50 cm long, dark at their bases and clad with dark brown scales. The **frond blade** is broadly triangular in outline, 25–90 cm long by 15–50 cm wide. It is twice- to three-times pinnate with the **pinnae** being widely spaced. The coarsely and sharply toothed **ultimate segments** have a netted pattern of veins near their midribs. The **sori** are situated in the notches around the margins but do not reach the tips of the segments. This is mainly a shade-loving fern and when growing in more open situations its fronds are usually rather yellowish instead of a pale green. It is confined to New Zealand.

Shaking brake *Pteris tremula*

Shaking brake is a rather common fern that occurs on the Kermadec and Three Kings Islands, throughout most of the North Island and in coastal areas of the South Island as far south as the Paringa River and Banks Peninsula. It does not occur in the central regions of the North Island. A handsome and graceful fern, it may be distinguished by its brown, polished stipes, long and narrow ultimate segments, on which the veins do not meet to form a netted pattern. It is a fern of tufted habit with a short and erect **rhizome**. Its **stipes** are 15–60 cm long, almost blackish towards the base and clad with dark brown scales. The **frond blade** is long-triangular, 30–90 cm long by 20–70 cm wide, bright green, and three- to four-times pinnate. Its **ultimate segments** are narrow with toothed margins and blunt tips, and are either shortly stalked or directly attached to the rib. The **sori** are more or less continuous around the margins but do not reach the tips of the segments. The shaking brake is more common in drier forests, scrublands or along open track and roadsides. Its fronds are unpalatable to stock and it can be quite common in areas that are heavily browsed by stock. It is also known as the tender brake and turawera.

Tangle fern *Gleichenia dicarpa*

Tangle fern is an interesting and unusual species that may be recognised because it forms dense, tangled masses of fronds that are repeatedly forked. The ultimate frond segments are quite fine, being very narrow with their margins rolled downwards to create the appearance of being small, open pouches. It has a far-creeping **rhizome** and in some places covers quite large areas with its tangled masses. The smooth and slender **stipes** are a rich red-brown. Its **fronds** are forked several times with their branches spreading in a horizontal plane. In favourable situations the fronds may be up to 1 m tall, although often they are only about

60 cm or so. They are dull green above, often whitish beneath and quite harsh to the touch. Its **pinnae** are 2–5 cm long, narrow and with 20–50 **ultimate segments** which are closely set. On the undersides of the segments one or two **sporangia** are tucked into the pouch that is created by the rounded and down-rolled margins. Tangle fern can be found in the North, South, Stewart and Chatham Islands in lowland to subalpine regions; in heathlands and boggy ground, usually on poorly drained clay soils. It is more common in the North Island and rarer in eastern areas. The species is also known as spider fern and swamp umbrella fern. Outside of New Zealand it is quite widely distributed from Australia to Malaysia.

45

Carrier tangle *Gleichenia microphylla*

GLEICHENIACEAE

In many respects carrier tangle is similar to *G. dicarpa*, the most obvious differences being in the ultimate segments which are flattened, not pouch-like, and are also tri-angular in shape. Each small segment has two to four sporangia instead of the one to two of the tangle fern. Its larger fronds are more forked and, when scrambling through scrub, may be up to 2 m or more tall. The **stipes** are smooth or scaly, rich reddish brown and slender. Its **fronds** fork repeatedly, in one to three tiers, with the branches often much interlaced, light green above and pale beneath. The **pinnae** are 1–4 cm long. There are usually 30–50 **ultimate segments**, which are very close-set and about 3 mm long. They are either flat or just slightly curved downwards. There are two to four bright yellow **sporangia**. The carrier tangle occurs in lowland areas of the North, South and Stewart Islands, from North Cape southwards. It is absent from the eastern coasts of both main islands. It is more common in the northern part of the country and less common in the south. As with the tangle fern it generally occurs on poor clay soils, or on boggy land, in open country or among light and open low scrub. It is not uncommon around the thermal areas of the central North Island. The carrier tangle is also known as the parasol fern and waewaekaka.

Umbrella fern *Sticherus cunninghamii*

This is a distinct and very easily recognised species as well as being a very handsome fern. It may be identified by its regularly branched frond so that it is fan-shaped or somewhat like an umbrella. Particularly when growing on a bank, or around forest margins, the fronds are slanted obliquely, to one side, in a very distinctive manner. It occurs throughout the North, South and Stewart Islands, but is not common in the east and far south of the South Island. Umbrella fern is usually found in lowland to montane forests and in the North Island more often grows at higher altitudes. A common habitat for it is along roadside banks where it can form conspicuous colon-

ies. It also occurs on the floor of dry, open forests but the colonies are then often sparser than when it grows in better-lit situations. Its **rhizome** is widely creeping and bran-ched to form large colonies. The **stipes** are 20–50 cm long and pale brown, while the **frond blade** is fan-shaped and divided into a number of pairs, with the **pinnae** being 15–30 cm long. Its narrow **ultimate segments** are 1–2 cm long and usually have whitish or glaucous undersurfaces. The yellowish brown **sori** are numerous and pro-duced in a row either side of the midrib. On very large fronds **growths** may sprout from their centres so that there may be up to three or four superimposed branches. The umbrella fern is also known as waekura and tapuwae kotuku. The latter name means the 'footprint of the white heron' and refers to the appearance of the frond.

Sticherus flabellatus

This is a lovely fern of a very distinctive appearance and it is easily recognised by its attractive, deep green, fan-shaped fronds. It occurs in the North Island from North Cape to the Bay of Plenty and in the South Island from north-west Nelson to northern Westland. In the North Island it often grows in short scrub on open hillsides; it is not uncommon on gumlands near Spirits Bay and is also plentiful around the Keri- keri Falls. At the southern limit of its range and in the South Island it tends to favour streamsides in lowland forests and scrub. It also occurs on Great Barrier and Great Mercury Islands. Its stout **rhizome** is branched and may be up to 6 mm in diameter. The smooth and polished **stipes** are pale brown and 20–40 cm long. The **blade of the frond** is once- or twice-branched with each branch forking two to three times. Sometimes the branches are superimposed in two or three tiers. The **pinnae** are 10–30 cm long and the **ultimate segments** are 3–5 cm long by about 3 mm wide. Its yellowish brown **sori** are copiously produced in a single row each side of the midrib of the segment. *Sticherus flabellatus* also occurs in Australia, New Cale- donia and New Guinea.

Comb fern *Ctenopteris heterophylla*

Comb fern is a very distinctive little fern that is usually found growing as an epiphyte on tree trunks, tree fern trunks or, more rarely, on rocks and banks. It forms small tufts or clumps and is recognised by its fronds being distinctively lobed with the lobes being arranged, along either side of the midrib, like the teeth of a comb. It has a tufted **rhizome** from which the fronds usually hang down. The **stipes** are rather short and winged. The fronds are quite variable in size and shape, deep green and rather leathery in texture and when dry tend to curl. The **blades of the fronds** are 4–30 cm long by 5 mm to 7 cm wide with the **ultimate segments** being variously toothed. The comb fern can be found in the North, South and Stewart Islands as well as on the Chatham and Auckland Islands. It occurs in lowland forests and subalpine scrub and attains its finest development in the moister forests. In more exposed situations it may be quite stunted. It is also known as the perching polypody, and also occurs in Australia.

49

Strap ferns *Grammitis* species

This is a group of small, tufted ferns that have narrow, strap-like, undivided fronds. In New Zealand there are 10 species, ranging from some having fronds up to 22 cm long to the most diminutive with fronds no more than 3 cm in length. In general, they all tend to have a rather similar appearance, the differences between the species being mainly of a botanical nature. One of the commoner species is *C. billardierei*, which has **fronds** 3–20 cm long by 3–9 mm wide, blunt at their tips. The two to 27 pairs of **sori** are arranged in a characteristic herringbone fashion. It is common throughout the North, South, Stewart and Chatham Islands, and also extends to the subantarctic islands. It occurs in lowland forests and subalpine scrub generally as a low epiphyte, on rocks or sometimes on the ground. On the ground it is usually to be found growing in the fibrous root masses that occur at the bases of certain trees. At the other end of the scale is the smallest species, *C. poeppigiana*. It forms small mats on rocks, mainly in alpine or subalpine areas and, unless examined closely, would not be recognised as a fern. Its **fronds** are no more than 5–30 mm long by 2–5 mm wide and have very blunt tips. Usually they are at the smaller end of the scale. It occurs in mountain areas throughout the North, South and Stewart Islands and extends down to Macquarie Island in the subantarctic. (*C. billardierei* is illustrated.)

Lance fern *Anarthropteris lanceolata*

Lance fern is easily recognised by its bright green, long and narrow, strap-shaped fronds that have rather large oval sori on their undersurfaces. It grows on tree trunks, rocks and banks in lowland and coastal forests throughout the North Island. In the South Island it is less common, except in Nelson and Westland, and occurs as far south as Greymouth on the western side and to Banks Peninsula on the east. Generally, it seldom occurs very far above ground level. It has a creeping **rhizome** that may cover quite large areas with a netted pattern. The **frond** is 7–30 cm long by 7 mm to 2.3 cm wide, is quite sharply pointed and has a somewhat fleshy texture. The oval **sori** are large for the size of the frond and are produced in a single row either side of the midrib and produce small bumps on the upper surface of the frond. It is particularly abundant in the Auckland district, often covering rocks and tree trunks with a green tapestry. This fern is quite sensitive to dry conditions and will soon commence to wilt if there is insufficient moisture. The lance fern belongs to one of New Zealand's few endemic fern genera.

Kowaowao *Microsorum pustulatum*

Kowaowao is a common fern occurring in a wide variety of habitats and having a range of frond shapes that can be quite bewildering, especially as the differing frond shapes can occur on the one plant. Its **rhizomes** are widely creeping, about pencil thickness, pale greenish and liberally spotted with small, dark scales. The pale brown **stipes** are smooth and shiny, and 2–25 cm long. The **frond blades** are very variable in shape; on smaller plants they are usually strap-shaped and undivided (7–25 cm by 1–3 cm), while on larger plants they may vary from being simply lobed (just one or two lobes) to having up to 12 pairs of lobes. The larger fronds are then from 6–45 cm long by 4–30 cm wide. The **sori** are large, orange-red and situated between the margin and the midrib. Their presence is usually indicated by the bumps that they create on the upper surface. Some fertile fronds that produce numerous sori have very narrow segments and have the appearance of being a different species. The kowaowao is abundant throughout New Zealand and may be found creeping over the ground, on rocks or epiphytic on trees in coastal to montane forests, scrub and open areas. Usually, it occurs in slightly drier places. It also occurs on the Chatham Islands and in the subantarctic. It is also known as hound's tongue, maratata and paraharaha. Botanically, it has had a number of names, formerly being known as *Phymatosorus pustulatus* and *P. diversifolius*.

Fragrant fern *Microsorum scandens*

Fragrant fern has a widely creeping, slender **rhizome** and commences life as a juvenile, growing on the ground. At that stage its simple, strap-shaped fronds may be from 10–30 cm long by up to 2 cm wide. Once it commences to climb a tree it then begins to assume its adult form with the fronds becoming larger; gradually it changes shape with up to 20 pairs of lobes. The pale brown **stipes** are 3–10 cm long. The adult **frond blade** is 20–50 cm long by 5–18 cm wide, and a dull, dark green with smooth margins to the lobes. Especially in the adult form it is a graceful and attractive fern. Its **sori** are rather small and situated near to the margins. They are sunk into a shallow cavity, which shows as a bump on the upper surface. It is also known as moki and was formerly used by Maori for making scented sachets, being mixed with oil and other scented plant products. The scented fern occurs in the North and South Islands as well as on the Chatham Islands. In the North Island it is abundant in coastal and lowland

forests from North Cape southwards, usually preferring moister habitats. In the South Island it occurs in Marlborough, Nelson and Westland to about as far south as Franz Josef. It is rare on the eastern coast. Fragrant fern was known as *Phymatosorus pustulatus* and *P. scandens*.

Juvenile.

53

Leather-leaf fern *Pyrrosia elaeagnifolia*

POLYPODIACEAE

This is an easily recognised fern even though the shape of its **fronds** is rather variable. It may be recognised by its tough and leathery fronds that are rather fleshy and vary from being rounded or spoon-shaped to long and spatula-shaped. They are deep green above and densely covered with brownish or buff-coloured hairs on their undersurfaces. The fronds vary from 3–20 cm long by 1–2 cm wide. The leather-leaf fern commonly grows on trees, particularly the higher branches, or on rocks. It occurs throughout the Kermadec, Three Kings, North, South, Stewart and Chatham Islands, being common in coastal, lowland and montane regions. It is commonly seen on native trees but also on a range of introduced trees including pine and *Cupressus macrocarpa*. In coastal areas it will grow on exposed rock, sometimes in full sun. It has a widely creeping **rhizome** and will cover large areas of its host tree. The large **sori** are medium brown and, at maturity, sometimes almost completely cover the undersurfaces of the fronds. The longer and narrow fronds are the fertile ones while the smaller, rounded fronds are barren. This is a very tough and adaptable fern that will withstand prolonged dry conditions. The fern was formerly known as *P. serpens*, a species now known to be confined to the Pacific Islands.

Hymenophyllum bivalve

This is one of the medium-sized and beautiful filmy ferns that usually grows on the ground. It has long-creeping **rhizomes** that grow through the debris and root fibres of the forest floor. Its **stipes** are 3–15 cm long, smooth and wiry and black to very dark brown. The **frond blade** is broadly triangular or broadly oval, 6–20 cm long by 3–16 cm wide and is a lovely bright green. It is three- to four-times pinnate and the **ultimate segments** are quite finely cut and their margins have a few fine teeth around them (requiring a hand lens to see them). The **sori** are produced at the tips of the ultimate segments. Identifying characters for this species are that it is the largest of those that have toothed margins, and the much-divided nature of the frond, which is generally broadly triangular. *Hymenophyllum bivalve* occurs in the North, South, Stewart and Chatham Islands in lowland to montane forests, from the Thames area southwards, but is uncommon north of Lake Taupo. In the South Island it often carpets quite large areas of ground in the higher-altitude beech forests. It occurs from sea level to 900 m.

Irirangi is probably the commonest of the filmy ferns, being found in most wetter forests throughout the country. It more commonly grows on the ground but also grows on banks and as an epiphyte on trees. Its wiry **rhizomes** are wide-spreading and it often covers extensive areas of the forest floor. The **stipes** are 4–17 cm long, dark and shiny. Its **frond blades** are triangular to narrow-triangular and when growing on the ground are either erect or curving. With plants growing on banks or trees they are usually more drooping. They are three- to four-times pinnate and are usually of a deep green colour. A mixture of the pale green young fronds among the older ones creates a lovely effect. The margins of the **ultimate segments** are smooth and the prominent **sori** are situated on their tips. Except in the drier forests along the eastern side of the South Island, *H. demissum* is common throughout the Kermadec, North, South, Stewart and Chatham Islands. It also extends down to the Auckland Islands. Irirangi occurs in lowland to lower montane forests. It is also known as piripiri (a name that applies to a number of different plants) and drooping filmy fern.

Matua mauku *Hymenophyllum dilatatum*

This veritable giant among the filmy ferns is the largest of the native species. It is very easily recognised by the length of its fronds, the great width of its ultimate segments and the quite distinct wing that extends along either side of the midrib and the stipes. *Hymenophyllum dilatatum* has long and relatively stout creeping **rhizomes** but seldom forms very large colonies. The **stipes** are 2–15 cm long and narrowly winged almost to their bases. Its **frond blades** are ovate to narrowly oblong, 8–40 cm long by 4–15 cm wide, bright jade-green, broadly winged along the midrib and are three- to four-times pinnate. The **ultimate segments** are about 3 mm wide, have smooth margins with the **sori** slightly immersed into their tips. It occurs throughout the North, South, Stewart and Chatham Islands in lowland to lower montane forests, but is

absent from the drier eastern side of the South Island except for Banks Peninsula. Its distribution ranges from sea level to 900 m. Matua mauku is confined to New Zealand. It is usually epiphytic on the branches of trees or on fallen trees and, in such situations, attains its maximum size. When growing on banks or similar situations its fronds are often much shorter. Unlike some filmy ferns this species generally seems to prefer darker situations.

HYMENOPHYLLACEAE

Rusty filmy fern *Hymenophyllum ferrugineum*

This is a distinct and easily recognised species. It is a medium-sized fern and is one of only two species that have their fronds densely covered with hairs. The fronds are an unusual colour, being dull green tinged with brown. *Hymenophyllum ferrugineum* has a thin, creeping **rhizome** and sometimes forms quite large patches or colonies. Its slender **stipes** are 2–8 cm long and are clad with scattered hairs that eventually fall off. The **frond blade** is 5–20 cm long by 2–5 cm wide, narrowly ovate to oblong and two- to three-times pinnate. Its **ultimate segments** are crowded, with smooth margins, and have the **sori** sunk into their tips. This fern occurs in the North, South and Stewart Islands. In the North Island it is common in lowland to lower montane forests from Kaitaia southwards. In the South Island it is rare and local on the eastern side. The plant mainly grows as an epiphyte in wet forests, on trees and especially tree ferns. Occasionally, it will also grow on rocks and banks. Its partiality for growing on tree fern trunks is possibly due to the fact that they usually remain more consistently moist than tree trunks. *Hymenophyllum ferrugineum* ranges from sea level to 800 m. The species also occurs in South America.

Hymenophyllum flabellatum

Hymenophyllum flabellatum is another species that is fairly easily recognised, the fan-shaped primary segments of its fronds making it quite distinct, and it is also quite partial to growing on tree fern trunks. Its **rhizomes** are widely spreading. The slender **stipes** are 2–12 cm long, smooth and polished. The narrow **frond blades** are 2–25 cm long by 1.5–6 cm wide and are two- to three-times pinnate. Usually, they are an attractive pale to medium green. The **primary segments** are generally fan-shaped and more or less overlap each other. The **ultimate segments** have smooth margins and the **sori** are at the tips of the individual segments. The size of the fronds can be quite variable and, even on the one tree, it is possible to find larger fronds and small, stunted fronds close together. The fern occurs on the Kermadec Islands, North, South, Stewart and Chatham Islands, and extends down to the subantarctic islands. Generally, it is common throughout most of the country except for the drier areas along the east of the South Island. It grows in lowland and lower montane forests, occasionally on overhanging banks and rocks, and ranges from sea level to 800 m. It also occurs in Australia, and some Pacific Islands.

The conspicuous, crinkly or crimped wing along either side of the midrib and the stipes makes this an easily recognised species. In fact, it is the only native species to have such a feature. It occurs throughout the North Island in lowland to montane forests and in the South Island in lowland forests, mainly in the wetter western areas, but is absent from the drier eastern areas. It also occurs on the Chatham Islands. *Hymenophyllum flexuosum* mostly grows on rock in stream gullies but may occasionally grow as an epiphyte on trees. Its **rhizomes** are quite wide-creeping. The **stipes** are 3–11 cm long with broad, crinkly wings almost to their bases. The triangular **frond blade** is 6–25 cm long by 3–12 cm wide, bright green but darkening with age, and is three- to four-times pinnate. The **ultimate segments** have smooth margins with the **sori** terminating the individual segments, either singly or in pairs. Only one other species (*H. atrovirens*) has a similar wing along its midrib and stipes, but it is not crinkled, its fronds are smaller and it is much less common.

Hymenophyllum malingii is a most curious filmy fern because it does not appear to be filmy and because the ultimate segments have a tubular appearance instead of being flattened, as with other species. In addition, the whole frond blade is covered with a dense covering of hairs that gives it a brownish grey or grey-green colour. Once seen it cannot be mistaken for any other species. A further interesting feature of this fern is that it is almost entirely confined to the trunks of the mountain cedar (*Libocedrus bidwillii*), although, on rare occasions, it will grow on *Dacrydium* or *Nothofagus*. Its favourite site is on dead or decaying trunks of *Libocedrus*. It rarely grows on living trees and, if it does, it is always where there is a dead area on the trunk. Its long, thin **rhizomes** seek out cracks and fissures in the dead wood and will form quite dense colonies. The thread-like **stipes** are 3–10 cm long. Its rather narrow **frond blades** are 5–20 cm long by 1–3 cm wide, and are two- to three-times pinnate. The **ultimate segments** are linear, rounded and appear to be cut off more or less square across their tips; the **sori** are at the tips of the segments. The fern can be found in montane to subalpine forests of the North Island from Te Aroha and the Ruahine Range southwards, and in the South Island from north-western Nelson to South Westland and also near Dunedin. It also occurs in Tasmania.

61

HYMENOPHYLLACEAE

A small- to medium-sized filmy fern that has a wide range of habitats from lowland forests to alpine scrub and rock outcrops. It has far-spreading **rhizomes** and will form large colonies on the forest floor or, when on alpine rocks, more compact clumps. The slender **stipes** are 2–10 cm long. Its **frond blades** are narrowly rounded or triangular, 3–20 cm long by 1.5–10 cm wide, and are three- to four-times pinnate. They are a fresh green to deep green, and on alpine rocks are often a dark olive green. Its **ultimate segments** are narrow with toothed margins and the one to several quite large **sori** are usually produced towards the bases of the segments. *Hymenophyllum multifidum* is found throughout the North, South, Stewart and Chatham Islands and also extends down to the sub-antarctic islands. It is often common in lowland to subalpine forests and subalpine scrub, growing on the ground and rocks or as an epiphyte on trees. It ascends to 1310 m and in the alpine zone may occur on shady, overhanging banks in tussock grassland or herbfields, or in clefts on shady rock outcrops. This fern is confined to New Zealand.

Hymenophyllum rarum

This is a delicate little filmy fern, its name referring to the thin texture of its fronds and not to the rarity of its occurrence. Its **rhizome** is much-branched and is very thin. The black, hair-like **stipes** have a very delicate appearance and are 2–7 cm long. Its narrow **frond blade** is 2–12 cm long by 1–3 cm wide, twice-pinnate, and is a most unusual pale milky-green; in fact it is the only native filmy fern to have fronds of such a colour. The **ultimate segments** are  oblong with smooth margins and the **sori** terminate individual segments. *Hymenophyllum rarum* occurs in the North, South, Stewart and Chatham Islands, and also extends down to Auckland Islands. It occurs from Mangonui and Kaitaia southwards and, except for the drier eastern South Island, it is common in lowland to montane forests throughout. As well as being epiphytic on trees it also grows on moist banks and rocks, and, at times, even on exposed rocks. For a species that appears to be so delicate, as well as for a filmy fern, it has an amazing tolerance of dry conditions. When other species of filmy fern have been affected by drought *H. rarum* may appear to be quite unaffected.

HYMENOPHYLLACEAE

Compared with the giant *H. dilatatum*, this is one of the smaller species of filmy fern and is often quite diminutive. Although its fronds may be up to 9 cm in length, they are probably more frequently within the range of 2–3 cm long. It occurs throughout the North Island, along the western side of the South Island, extending out to Dunedin, and then on Stewart and Chatham Islands and is fairly common in moist lowland to montane forests. It usually forms matted patches on tree trunks, fallen logs and on rocks. *Hymenophyllum revolutum* is generally regarded as one of the commonest of the native filmy ferns. It is usually recognised by its small size and the toothed margins of the frond segments and, being so small and matted, it could be mistaken for a moss. Its thread-like **rhizome** is much-branched and quite wide-spreading. The **stipes** are thin and wiry and 5–30 mm long. The narrow **frond blade** is 1–9 cm long by 5–20 mm wide, medium green and two- to three-times pinnate. Its **ultimate segments** are narrow and have distinctly toothed margins. The **sori** are produced on short segments close to the midrib. It is distinguished from two similar species by the midrib of the frond being partially winged.

Piripiri *Hymenophyllum sanguinolentum*

Piripiri is a medium-sized species that is common throughout much of New Zealand. It occurs in a variety of habitats, from forests to rock faces. It has a much-branched **rhizome** and will form quite large, matted colonies. Its blackish **stipes** may have a few hairs at their bases and be narrowly winged in their upper parts (a pocket lens is needed). The **frond blades** are 5–25 cm long by 3–12 cm wide, often curved, deep green and three- to four-times pinnate. The **ultimate segments** are quite crowded, giving the frond a thick appearance, and have smooth margins. The **sori** are produced on short segments on the upper portion of the frond. Piripiri occurs on the Three Kings Islands, as well as in the North, South and Stewart Islands and on the Chatham Islands. It is most common in lowland and montane forests, either on the ground or as an epiphyte on trees. It also grows on rocks, sometimes in rather exposed conditions, and is generally quite a drought-tolerant species. It ranges from sea level to 900 m. *Hymenophyllum sanguinolentum* is also known as the scented fern because its fronds are somewhat scented, when dry. *H. villosum* is a very similar species, distinguished by having distinctly hairy stipes. In the South and Stewart Islands it may occur more in montane forests.

As well as being one of the largest of our filmy ferns, *Hymenophyllum scabrum* is also one of the most handsome. It is very easily recognised because of the dense covering of rough, bristly hairs on its stipes and the olive-green colour of the frond blades. The blackish **stipes** are 4–15 cm long and the hairs are often pale to somewhat reddish in colour. Its **frond blades** are 10–40 cm long by 5–14 cm wide, narrowly triangular and three- to four-times pinnate. The **ultimate segments** are linear with smooth margins and the **sori** terminate individual segments. *Hymenophyllum scabrum* is distributed through the North, South, Stewart and Chatham Islands and is fairly common except on the drier eastern side of the South Island. It generally grows in lowland to montane forests, as an epiphyte on trees and fallen logs or on the ground, but mostly on tree trunks. This fern is distributed from about Hokianga and Mangonui southwards and ranges from sea level to about 900 m. It is confined to New Zealand.

Kidney fern *Trichomanes reniforme*

The kidney fern is easily recognised by its distinctively shaped fronds and is surely one of the most remarkable and beautiful ferns in the world. It is endemic to New Zealand and is usually abundant in moist lowland to montane forests throughout the North Island, along the western side of the South Island and thence onto Stewart and the Chatham Islands. On the drier eastern side of the South Island it is rare and local. While it is mainly a terrestrial fern, it not infrequently adorns the lower branches of forest trees. Its **rhizome** is far-creeping and often covers quite large areas to form extensive mats on the forest floor. The wiry **stipes** are 5–25 cm long and erect. Its undivided **frond blade** is kidney-shaped, 3–10 by 4–13 cm and has smooth margins. It is a most beautiful translucent green, particularly when seen against the light. The **sori** are set around the upper margin of the frond blade and resemble a row of little pegs. For what is normally a denizen of moist forests, it is most unusual to find it growing on the exposed lava fields of Rangitoto Island, in the Hauraki Gulf. Kidney fern is also known as raurenga, konehu and kopakopa.

The *Trichomanes* species (other than the kidney fern) are collectively known as bristle ferns because of the bristle that protrudes from the trumpet-shaped receptacle containing the sporangia. This distinguishes them from the genus *Hymenophyllum*. *Trichomanes venosum* is perhaps the commonest species and is found in moist forests throughout the country. It has thread-like, much-branched **rhizomes** and usually forms quite dense colonies. The quite delicate **stipes** are 1–5 cm long. Its relatively narrow **frond blades** are 2–14 cm long by 1–5 cm wide and are a lovely pale, translucent green. The **ultimate segments** are often lobed at their bases. Its solitary **sori** are produced on the upper margins of the ultimate segments. It is often abundant in the wetter, montane to lower montane forests of the North, South and Stewart Islands, and ranges from sea level to 1100 m. It occurs only locally along the dry eastern side of the South Island. The fern is also found on the Kermadec and Chatham Islands, as well as in Tasmania and mainland Australia. It mainly grows on the matted trunks of tree ferns but will grow on tree trunks and occasionally on rocks.

Wheki ponga *Dicksonia fibrosa*

Wheki ponga is one of the most easily recognised species of tree fern. It is very distinctive with its thick, sturdy **trunk** covered with densely matted, fibrous roots, and the prominent **skirt** or investment of dead fronds that gird its trunk just below the crown of fronds. Usually, one glance at these characters is sufficient to identify it. It ranges from sea level to 760 m, and grows in lowland, hilly and lower montane forests in the North Island from Tauranga and the mid-Waikato southwards. In the South Island it is more common from the Marlborough Sounds and down the western side of the island, being local in the drier eastern areas. It also occurs on the Chatham Islands. The wheki ponga has a **trunk** 30–60 cm or more in diameter in its lower part. Generally, the **fronds** form a vase-shaped crown and the individual fronds are from 1.2–2.4 m long by 40–60 cm wide. They are quite harsh to the touch, but not as harsh as *D. squarrosa*. The upper surfaces of the fronds are green to dark green and shiny. On fertile fronds

their undersurfaces are covered with numerous brown **sori**, grouped around the margins of the frond segments, causing them to become strongly down-rolled. Maori used to use the trunks of wheki ponga for the construction of food storehouses, because the thick, fibrous trunks made them almost impenetrable to rats. The early European settlers also used them for the construction of bush huts.

DICKSONIACEAE

This is an unusual species because it occurs in two distinct forms. In the kauri forests of Northland, from about Whangarei northwards, it grows on short, erect, rather slender **trunks** up to about 2 m tall, while southwards from there, it has a branching **prostrate stem** that grows along the ground and forms low, trunkless colonies. Its slender **stipes** are smooth, pale-brown and densely clad with brown hairs at their bases. The **fronds** are few in number, 75 cm to 2 m long by 30–90 cm wide, smooth, yellowish to light-green above, paler beneath and three- to four-times pinnate. The dead fronds soon fall from the trunk. The **ultimate segments** are closely placed and on fertile fronds are covered with numerous **sori**. *Dicksonia lanata* ranges from sea level to 700 m or more, and occurs in the North Island from North Cape to the Tararua Range, although it is rather rare in the southern North Island. In the South Island it is found from the Marlborough Sounds to about Franz Josef, on the west. This fern grows in lowland to montane forests and in the South Island mainly occurs at higher altitudes.

Trunk and stipes.

Wheki *Dicksonia squarrosa*

Wheki is probably the most abundant of the native tree ferns and is found in forest areas throughout most of the country. Its main distinguishing characters are its slender black trunk from which project the hard, black bases of the old frond stalks, and the top of its trunk usually (but not always) being girdled with a dense **skirt**, or investment, of dead fronds. Its trunk may be up to 7 m tall. The **stipes** are densely covered with long, brownish black hairs. Its **fronds** are 1.2–2.4 m long by 60 cm to 1 m wide, dark green above and paler beneath. The undersurfaces of the fertile fronds are often so densely covered with **sori** that they cause the margins of the **ultimate segments** to roll strongly downwards. Wheki is abundant in lowland and hilly forests throughout the North, South and Stewart Islands from sea level to 760 m. It often sends out underground **rhizomes** that produce new plants so that it frequently grows in groves or colonies. After the forest has been cleared it can be one of the principal regenerative plants. It is also known as the slender tree fern and tirawa.

Stipes.

71

Creepin g tree fern *Cyathea colensoi*

CYATHEACEAE

To refer to this species as a tree fern is rather a misnomer because it rarely has an erect trunk, the **stem** or **trunk** usually being quite prostrate and rooting into the ground. When it does grow erect its trunk may be up to 1 m tall. Its slender **stipes** are roughened and, especially towards their bases, are covered with pale to reddish, chaffy scales. The **frond blade** is up to 1.5 m long by 50–60 cm wide, has a soft texture, yellowish to deep green above, and is three-times pinnate. Its old fronds soon fall away and decay. The **ultimate segments** are sharply toothed with numerous **sori** on the fertile fronds. *Cyathea colensoi* is purely a species of cool, mountain forests and is found in the North, South and Stewart Islands from about Mt Hikurangi southwards; it is rare on the dry eastern side of the South Island. It ranges from 600–1200 m. It is

often mistaken for young plants of the whe (*C. smithii*); however, a search around the base of *C. colensoi* will soon reveal the prostrate stem that the former never has. The creeping tree fern is also known as the mountain tree fern and the golden tree fern.

Stipes.

Gully fern *Cyathea cunninghamii*

Gully fern is a graceful species of tree fern, rather similar to the mamaku but may be recognised by its more slender trunk and less robust fronds that form a smaller crown. It is nowhere common and is usually only observed as scattered populations. Its **trunk** may be up to 20 m tall, but is generally shorter, and is furnished with the dark brown appressed bases of the old stipes. The **stipes** are slender, blackish brown and lack the really thickened bases of *C. medullaris*. Its **frond blades** are up to 3 m long by 60 cm to 1.2 m wide and are three- to four-times pinnate. The **ultimate segments** are sharply toothed around their margins and have numerous **sori**. It is an emergent tree fern, and its crown of shorter, stiffer fronds gives it a distinctive silhouette when it is seen standing well above the surrounding trees. The gully fern occurs from Kaitaia to Wellington in the North Island, being only locally common in the moister western areas. In the South Island local populations of it occur from the Marlborough Sounds to Nelson and then down the west coast to South Westland. It also occurs on the Chatham Islands. It grows in coastal, lowland and montane forests, usually favouring damp gullies and river banks. The gully fern is also known as the slender tree fern and punui.

Silver tree fern *Cyathea dealbata*

As well as being one of the most distinctive of our tree ferns it is also most easily recognised. The silvery-white undersides of its fronds serve to immediately identify it. Its **trunk** is up to 10 m tall and about 45 cm in diameter at the base. It is fibrous with matted aerial roots and the upper part is marked by the bases of the old frond stalks. It has numerous fronds that usually spread more or less horizontally. The rather slender **stipes** are covered with a silvery-white, waxy bloom. Its **fronds** are 2–4 m long by 60 cm to 1.2 m wide with deep green upper surfaces and they are three-times pinnate. The old fronds soon fall to leave a clean trunk. On very young

plants the undersurfaces of the fronds are usually green because they do not develop their distinctive silvery-white colour until they are several years old. The undersurfaces of fertile fronds are dotted with numerous brown **sori**. The silver tree fern is common in lowland to montane forests throughout the North and South Islands to about as far south as the Catlins area on the east and to about Karamea on the west. It also occurs on the Three Kings and Chatham Islands. An alternative name is ponga, which is also a generic vernacular name for tree ferns in general. The Maori name of ponga has become corrupted into 'punga' and, sometimes 'bungie'.

Undersurface of pinna.

CYATHEACEAE

74

As well as being the tallest of our tree ferns, the mamaku is also the noblest. With its tall, slender trunk and huge crown of fronds it is easily recognised. The more or less hexagonal scars that the fallen fronds leave on its trunk and the exceptionally thick, black bases of the **stipes** are generally sufficient to identify it. Its **trunk** may be up to 20 m tall and about 60 cm in diameter at its thickened base, but more slender higher up. It has 20 to 30 **fronds**, slightly curving and from 2.5–6 m long by up to 2 m wide. Their upper surfaces are dark green and shiny and the undersurfaces pale. On fertile fronds their undersurfaces are dotted with innumerable dark brown **sori**. The

mamaku is found from sea level to 600 m in lowland and hilly forests throughout the North Island and in the South Island from the Marlborough Sounds and Nelson to southern Fiordland, on the west. On the east it extends to about Kaikoura, is rare on Banks Peninsula and is found sparingly in eastern Otago. It also occurs on the Three Kings, Stewart and Chatham Islands. Mamaku is also known as korau and black tree fern, while in Westland it is known as the king fern.

Young crook or crozier.

Whe *Cyathea smithii*

This beautiful tree fern is abundant in damp, lowland and montane forests in the North, South and Stewart Islands, from Kaitaia southwards. It ranges from sea level to 600 m and is usually the dominant tree fern in the cooler forests of higher altitudes. Being found on the Auckland Islands, it also has the distinction of having the southernmost distribution of any tree fern. Its thick, fibrous **trunk** is up to 8 m tall and about 23 cm in diameter. The **fronds** spread horizontally and are from 1.5–2.7 m long by 45–75 cm wide. Their upper surfaces are a bright, fresh green and the undersurfaces are paler. On fertile fronds the small, numerous **sori** are dark brown. A distinguishing feature of this species is the **skirt** or investment of the old frond midribs that hang down from just below the crown. If any further confirmation is required the chestnut-brown scales that clothe the lower portion of the stipes and the straw-coloured, soft, woolly scales at their bases should be sufficient. The whe is also known as the soft tree fern and katote.

Feather fern *Pneumatopteris pennigera*

This handsome species is common throughout most of New Zealand, being found in damp, lowland forests in the North and South Islands as well as occurring on the Three Kings and Chatham Islands. The **rhizomes** of older plants may grow erect into short trunks up to 60 cm tall, topped by a crown of fronds. Its pale-brown **stipes** are 5–25 cm long. The **fronds** are 30 cm to 1.5 m long by 10–40 cm wide, dark green above and of a thin texture. They have a symmetrical appearance, enriched by dark brown midribs, while the main segments are conspicuously veined. Copious small **sori** are produced in two rows close to the midribs of the segments. The feather fern is abundant, particularly along streamsides and in damp gullies, often in heavy shade, and it ranges from sea level to 700 m. In the South Island it is often absent from the drier eastern parts, while in southern areas it is largely confined to coastal regions. It also occurs in eastern Australia. The feather fern is also known as the gully fern, piupiu and pakauroharoha.

Loxsoma cunninghamii

LOXSOMATACEAE

Loxsoma cunninghamii is an uncommon and lovely fern that is the sole species of a genus confined to New Zealand. It has quite long and stout, creeping **rhizomes** and forms small to largish colonies. The polished **stipes** are light to dark brown and 20–60 cm long. Its **frond blades** are distinctively broadly triangular, 20–60 cm long by 15–40 cm wide, the upper surface light green to yellowish green, the under-

surface either milky-green or silvery-white, and they are three- to four-times pinnate. The **ultimate segments** are rather broad and toothed or notched around their margins. Its numerous **sporangia** are quite unusual in that they are produced from the notches of the ultimate segments as small protuberances. *Loxsoma* is found only in lowland forests in the northern part of the North Island from Mangonui

and Kaitaia southwards to Thames. It grows in clearings in tall manuka (*Leptospermum scoparium*) scrub forest or in open forest, usually on banks, alongside tracks, roadsides or along streams. Although not as common as formerly, it is still locally abundant in some localities. The broadly triangular frond is quite distinctive, whether it be the form with the silvery-white undersurface or the form that has the milky-green undersurface.

Form with silvery undersurface.

Water fern *Histiopteris incisa*

Water fern is a large and strong-growing species that is common throughout most of the country. Its wide-spreading **rhizome** often forms thickets or large colonies around the outskirts of forest or in open areas within the forest. It can be recognised by its rather coarsely cut, bright green fronds that have quite a soft texture. The **stipes** are 15–90 cm long, yellowish to reddish brown, erect and shiny, and sometimes becoming quite blackish at maturity. Its **frond blade** is more or less triangular, 25 cm to 1 m long by 15–75 cm wide, quite smooth, bluish green when young and becoming bright green with age, two- to three-times pinnate. **Ultimate segments** are rounded at their tips and with the **sori** almost continuous around their smooth margins. As well as occurring on the three main islands of New Zealand, it is also found on the Kermadec and Chatham Islands and extends down to some of the subantarctic islands. The water fern grows in lowland to subalpine regions, in clearings, open places, along roadsides, stream banks or in other disturbed habitats. It also grows around thermal areas. In warmer districts it tends to be evergreen, but becomes deciduous as it moves south. It is also found in the tropics and southern temperate regions.

This is another common fern that occurs throughout most of the country. It can be recognised by its quite soft, large and branching fronds of either a pale or mid-green. With its wide-spreading **rhizomes** it often forms large colonies, particularly around forest margins or in clearings. The **stipes** are 8–60 cm long, reddish brown at their bases and yellow-brown higher up. Its **frond blades** are broadly triangular, 20–90 cm long by 15–60 cm wide, and three- to four-times pinnate. **Ultimate segments** usually have rather blunt teeth around their margins; the **sori** are small and numerous in the notches around the margins. *Hypolepis ambigua* is distributed throughout lowland and lower montane forests of the North Island. In the South and Stewart Islands it is mainly confined to lowland and coastal areas. It also occurs on the Three Kings and the Chatham Islands. In addition it grows in scrub, open grasslands and even in boggy areas, and ranges from sea level to 600 m. This species was formerly known as *H. tenuifolia*.

Hypolepis distans

Hypolepis distans is a graceful fern of delicate appearance with its fronds forming either a tangled mass or scrambling up through associated vegetation. It is probably also the most distinctive of the native species of *Hypolepis*. Its creeping **rhizome** forms small colonies. The reddish brown **stipes** are 5–60 cm long, shiny, very slender and fragile. The narrow **frond blade** is 15–95 cm long by 9–40 cm wide, bright green to brownish green, with its primary segments quite widely spaced (hence its specific name); the **ultimate segments** are toothed or lobed and have the **sori** in their lower notches. *Hypolepis distans* is found throughout the North Island where it is common from Kaitaia to the Waikato region and less common southwards to Wellington. In the South Island it is locally common from the Marlborough Sounds to north-west Nelson and northern Westland, with only local occurrences elsewhere. It also occurs on Stewart and the Chatham Islands. The fern often grows in swampy areas, on decomposing logs and stumps in open forest or scrub, and on decaying tussocks or similar situations rich in humus.

Of the species of *Hypolepis* this one probably has the most finely and openly cut fronds, which gives it a beautiful and lacy texture. It is basically a mountain species, except in the far south of the South Island where it occurs at sea level. It is also one of the few native ferns that is completely deciduous in winter. Its **rhizome** is widely creeping and in some localities forms large colonies. The erect **stipes** are 5–35 cm long, yellowish brown to yellow-green, and shiny. Its **frond blades** are 15–70 cm long by 8–25 cm wide, broadly triangular and pale or light green. The **ultimate segments** are deeply and very finely cut, and the copious **sori** are produced near notches close to the upper margins of the segments. In the North Island it is found, in montane or subalpine regions, on the higher ranges from Mt Pirongia and the Raukumara Range southwards, while in the South Island it is widespread in most mountain areas, but descending to sea level in South Otago and Southland. It also occurs on Stewart and the Chatham Islands as well as on some of the subantarctic islands. The fern grows in a variety of habitats including open, rocky places, tussock grasslands, scrub and open forests, usually ranging from 150–1400 m. Before the fronds die down for winter they sometimes exhibit autumn colour by turning a soft yellow.

Sticky pig fern *Hypolepis rufobarbata*

Sticky pig fern is a fairly distinct species that may, usually, be recognised by its reddish purple stipes and midribs, and by the fact that its narrow fronds are often rather sticky (caused by minute glandular hairs) to the extent that small insects may become stuck to them. It has a creeping **rhizome**, and its **stipes** are 5–30 cm long, usually being clad with short and fine, but discernible, hairs. The **frond blade** is 6–50 cm long by 2–25 cm wide, softly hairy with minute hairs, and three-times pinnate. **Ultimate segments** are minutely hairy, especially around their margins. The **sori** are produced in two rows on each segment; rather closer to the centre vein than the margin. The sticky pig fern occurs in the North, South, Stewart and Chatham Islands. In the North Island it is rare in Northland, but becomes more common from Auckland to Wellington, usually in montane areas. In the South Island it can be common, in coastal and lowland areas, from Marlborough and Nelson and down the western side of the island while it is either rare or absent from the drier eastern side, particularly in South Canterbury and Central Otago. The fern usually grows on ground that has been disturbed, clay banks, stony ground along streams, or sometimes on rotting logs in forest and scrub. It ranges from sea level to 600 m.

Lace fern *Leptolepia novae-zelandiae*

This is a very distinct species that may be recognised by its elegant, finely cut fronds of a lace-like texture and its creeping habit. It is the only species of a genus that is confined to New Zealand. The fronds are quite widely spaced on its spreading **rhizome**. The **stipes** are reddish brown, 5–45 cm long, smooth and shiny. Its deep green **frond blades** are more or less triangular and 15–50 cm long by 6–30 cm wide. The **ultimate segments** are very fine and sharply pointed. The **sori** are numerous and are situated at the tips of the teeth of each segment. The lace fern is distributed in lowland forests of the North, South, Stewart and Chatham Islands from Kaitaia southwards. It ranges from sea level to 600 m, and mainly grows in cool and damp forests, but its distribution is often local. Sometimes it is also known by the inappropriate name of hare's-foot fern, presumably because it was once included in the genus *Davallia* (species of which are known by that name because the tips of their thick rhizomes are said to resemble a hare's foot).

Lindsaea linearis

This is a small fern that can be quite common in some areas but is not always easily noticed because it usually tends to hide itself under light manuka (*Leptospermum*) scrub or among other low vegetation. It has a creeping **rhizome** and forms small patches up to 30 cm in diameter or more. Its dark reddish brown **stipes** are 5–25 cm long, flexuous and wiry. The very narrow **frond blades** are a light to deepish green, 3–25 cm long by 5–15 mm wide and have 15 to 40 pairs of fan-shaped **segments**. On fertile fronds there are fewer segments. The margins of the segments on fertile fronds are slightly curled downwards. The **sori** form a continuous line along the upper margins of the segments. *Lindsaea linearis* occurs in coastal areas of the North, South, Stewart and Chatham Islands, as well as in Australia and New Caledonia. In the North Island it is common from North Cape to the Bay of Plenty, absent from much of the central North Island and then occurs around the Wellington region. In the South Island it is more local and occurs in northwest Nelson as well as in coastal regions of the southern part of the island. It usually grows on poor clay soils and boggy ground, especially under open manuka scrub or amid low grasses and similar vegetation. As one author puts it: 'this ... fern is no believer in self-advertisement' for it does not flaunt itself to the casual gaze.

Common lindsaea *Lindsaea trichomanoides*

Common lindsaea is a lovely little fern that always has very neat fronds and can usually be recognised by its reddish or chestnut-brown stipes and the broadly rounded tips of its ultimate segments. Its appearance can be rather variable, and the fronds of plants from northern regions are not as finely cut as those from the more southerly parts of its range. It has a creeping **rhizome** but, not infrequently, has the appearance of being a tufted plant. The **stipes** are 5–20 cm long and shiny. Its **frond blade** is 5–25 cm long by 2–8 cm wide, narrowly triangular to more or less oblong, green to dark green and two- to three-times pinnate at the base. There are five to 15 pairs of primary pinnae. The **ultimate segments** have rounded tips, broadest above the middle and with smooth or shallowly lobed margins. The **sori** form a continuous line around the outer margins of the segments. The common lindsaea grows on drier sites in lowland to montane open forests and scrublands, particularly on dry banks and the fibrous root mounds around large trees. The fern ranges from sea level to 700 m. It is found in the North, South and Stewart Islands but is not common in the eastern North Island. In the South Island it is confined to the Marlborough Sounds area and down through Westland to Fiordland.

Lace fern *Paesia scaberula*

This is a very common fern that is easily recognised by its extensive, creeping habit, delicate lace-like fronds of a rather harsh texture, and its zigzagging midribs. The lace fern is common, in lowland to montane areas, throughout the Three Kings, North, South, Stewart and Chatham Islands, ranging from sea level to 700 m. It usually grows in open places such as roadsides, track sides and in forest clearings, often forming dense masses to the exclusion of other vegetation. Sometimes it grows in more open forest but is then less vigorous. It often infests pastureland, forming large circular patches, which have earned it the name of ring fern. The **stipes** are 5–35 cm long and are usually a yellow-brown. The **frond blades** are 13–80 cm long by 7–35 cm wide, pale yellow-green and in spite of their delicate appearance are actually quite harsh to the touch. The **ultimate segments** are very narrow with copious **sori** extending along both margins but not reaching their apexes. The lace fern is variously known as pig fern, hard fern, scented fern and matata. The name of scented fern is derived from the fact that its fronds are quite strongly scented during warm weather.

Bracken *Pteridium esculentum*

The ubiquitous bracken needs no introduction. It is abundant in virtually every part of the country and, in some districts, is regarded as a serious weed of pasturelands. It has thick underground **rhizomes** that spread over great distances. Its stout and rigid **stipes** are 20 cm to 1 m or more long, shiny and pale chestnut-brown. The rigid **frond blades** are generally broadly triangular, 20 cm to 2 m long by 20 cm to 1.5 m wide, three- to four-times pinnate, and the upper surface is dark green and shiny. Its **ultimate segments** are quite narrow and usually slightly curved downwards. The **sori** usually extend right around the margins of the segments. Bracken is found in all islands of New Zealand, from the Kermadec group to the Chatham Islands and Antipodes Islands. It also occurs in south-eastern Asia, Australia and some of the Pacific islands. It extends from sea level to subalpine regions, usually growing in any open country, scrublands and around forest margins, ranging up to 1220 m. In some situations it will grow to about 4 m tall. Its thick and starchy underground rhizomes (known as aruhe) were a staple food of old-time Maori, particularly in times when other food sources were scarce. Bracken is also known as rahurahu, rarauhe and rarahu.

Hen and chickens fern *Asplenium bulbiferum*

This is a most beautiful and graceful fern that is common in almost any area of moist forest. It is usually easily recognised by the gemmae or little plantlets that develop along the upper surfaces of its fronds. In very moist conditions they can be most prolific. *Asplenium bulbiferum* grows from a stout, tufted **rhizome** that is covered with dark brown or blackish scales. Its **stipes** are 5–40 cm long, blackish brown at their bases and green above. The bright-green **frond blades** are 12 cm to 1.2 m long by 4–50 cm wide, two- to three-times pinnate and either more or less upright to somewhat drooping. Its **ultimate segments** can be very finely or more coarsely divided. The numerous **sori** are 2–5 mm long and produced either near to or along the margins of the seg-

ments. The fern occurs throughout the North, South, Stewart and Chatham Islands. It is common in any moist lowland to montane forest, particularly gullies and along stream courses, except in the drier eastern areas of the South Island such as the Canterbury Plains and inland Otago. When the fronds age and droop to the

ground the young plantlets (or gemmae) on them may take root and grow providing that there is sufficient light and clear space for them to survive. Hen and chickens fern is also known as manamana, mouku, mouki and mauku. The young crooks or croziers were formerly eaten by Maori.

Gemmae on the frond.

Necklace fern *Asplenium flabellifolium*

Necklace fern is a distinct and charming little fern that is quite different from the other native species of spleenwort. Although it has a tufted **rhizome**, the plant actually spreads to form quite large colonies by virtue of the extended midribs, at the tips of its prostrate fronds, being able to take root into the ground to form new plants. Its **stipes** are 1–15 cm long, slender, dark towards their bases and green above. The **frond blades** are 4–30 cm long by 8 mm to 4 cm wide, once-pinnate and bright to deep green. Its **ultimate segments** are distinctively fan-shaped with small teeth around their outer margins. There are several **sori** and they radiate outwards from the base of the segment. The necklace fern occurs quite widely, in lowland to montane areas, throughout the North and South Islands from North Cape to near Invercargill. It is more common from Hawke's Bay to about South Canterbury, and occurs mainly in eastern areas of both islands. It most frequently grows in dryish, rocky places as well as under open forest and scrub. It also occurs in Australia. The necklace fern is also known as butterfly fern, walking fern and rat-tail fern.

Drooping spleenwort *Asplenium flaccidum*

Although a common and quite variable species, in its larger forms drooping spleenwort is most distinct and easily recognised. It usually grows on trees and has long, drooping fronds that are fairly simply divided. It has a tufted **rhizome** from which the **stipes** are produced. They are 5–25 cm long, green and scaly at their bases. The **frond blade** is rather thick and leathery, 6 cm to 1 m long by 4–25 cm wide, dull green and twice pinnate. The **ultimate segments** are usually rather short and often resemble teeth on the primary pinnae rather than distinct segments. Its **sori** are produced very close to the margins of the segments and are up to 1 cm long. The drooping spleenwort occurs on all of the main islands of New Zealand from the Kermadec group to Stewart Island as well as on the Chatham and Snares Islands. It is common in lowland and montane forests throughout and is most commonly epiphytic on trees and tree ferns but also grows on rocks. In rocky scrub and pine forests it often grows as a terrestrial on the ground, particularly on the mounds around the bases of trees. These terrestrial forms usually have fairly erect, shorter fronds and do not much resemble the long, drooping, epiphytic plants. It is also known as raukatauri, makawe o raukatauri or hanging spleenwort. It is also found in Australia.

ASPLENIACEAE

Rocklax is a small and somewhat variable species with a rather delicate appearance. It exists in two main forms: one with the fronds having rounded ultimate segments and the other with very fine and narrower ultimate segments. This latter form was formerly recognised as a separate species (*A. colensoi*) but is now considered to be no more than a fine-leaved variant of *A. hookerianum*. The rocklax has a tufted **rhizome** from which arises the 1–20 cm green **stipes**. The deep green **frond blade** is 4–25 cm long by 1–15 cm wide, two- to three-times pinnate and has a somewhat rounded-oblong outline. Its **ultimate segments** have an open pattern and vary from being rounded to narrow and almost linear. Both variations are well marked as separate forms and usually do not occur together. Its **sori** are usually somewhat distant from the margins of the segments. This species is found in the North, South, Stewart and Chatham Islands but is rare in Northland and the King Country of the North Island, and also rare on the west coast of the South Island. Elsewhere it occurs in lowland and lower montane forests, often growing on clay banks, rock outcrops, rocky places and sometimes under light and open scrub. This species also occurs in Australia.

Asplenium lamprophyllum

Asplenium lamprophyllum is a very distinct native species of spleenwort, being the only one to have creeping and stoloniferous **rhizomes** so that it forms reasonably large colonies. The **stipes** are 6–20 cm long, brown at their bases and green above. Its **frond blades** are 15–60 cm long by 6–25 cm wide, widest about the middle and twice-pinnate. They are pale to medium green with a shiny upper surface (a feature that helps to distinguish it from

A. bulbiferum). The **ultimate segments** are deeply incised and have toothed margins. Its orange-brown **sori** are up to 1 cm long and nearer to the midrib than the margin. *Asplenium lamprophyllum* grows in coastal and lowland forests of the North Island, from North Cape to the King Country and Rotorua and then extends southwards to Wanganui, as local populations. It may form extensive colonies; often among rocks or on rocky ground and sometimes on clay banks. It is not dissimilar to *A. bulbiferum* but may be distinguished by its creeping (not tufted) habit, its shiny fronds and the absence of gemmae or plantlets on its fronds.

ASPLENIACEAE

Although by no means confined to them, *Asplenium lyallii* is mainly found growing on limestone rocks and calcareous soils. Generally, it can be recognised by its deep green, leathery fronds on which the lower (sometimes all) pinnae are lobed, or divided into secondary segments. It has a stout, tufted **rhizome** covered with blackish scales. Its **stipes** are 3–20 cm long and are green with brown bases. The **frond blades** are 4–40 cm long by 2–23 cm wide, dull and deep green to shiny or glossy, once- to twice-pinnately divided. Its **sori** are arranged in the typical herringbone pattern of spleenworts, up to 1 cm long, and do not reach the segment margins. *Asplenium lyallii* occurs through the North, South, Stewart and Chatham Islands from coastal and lowland areas to subalpine habitats. It is found mainly in the drier eastern areas of both main islands, but in the North Island it extends coastally to Port Waikato and Taranaki, while in the south it extends to Fiordland. Its usual habitats are in scrub and open forest and, in mountain areas, in rock crevices and under overhangs. In the Nelson area it is not uncommon to find it growing among the karren (fluted rock outcrops) in the karst landscape of Takaka Hill. It is rather variable in the size, colour and the amount of cutting on the frond segments. This fern is confined to New Zealand.

Shining spleenwort *Asplenium oblongifolium*

The shining spleenwort is one of the most handsome of the native species, its broad, glossy fronds serving at once to identify it. It has a thick **rhizome** that forms hard, rounded masses, clad on their tops with blackish scales. The **stipes** are 5–50 cm long, with dark brown bases and becoming green in their upper halves. The **frond blades** are 10 cm to 1 m long by 7–45 cm wide, drooping or arching and once-pinnate. Its **pinnae** have finely toothed margins and long, pointed tips. The **sori** are up to 3 cm long, arranged in herringbone fashion, and do not reach the margins. The shining spleenwort occurs on the Kermadec Islands, through much of the North Island and in coastal areas of the South Island as far south as Banks Peninsula on the east and to about Hokitika on the west. It also occurs on the Chatham Islands. The fern grows in shaded, lowland and lower montane forests, in open scrub and on exposed coastal cliffs. Although principally a terrestrial species, it sometimes grows as a low epiphyte on trees. It is confined to New Zealand. The shining spleenwort is also known as huruhuru whenua, paranako and paretao.

Shore spleenwort *Asplenium obtusatum*

Shore spleenwort is somewhat similar to the shining spleenwort but differs in having thick, fleshy fronds with usually rather rounded tips to its pinnae. As with the previous species its **rhizome** forms a thick and rounded mass, above ground, and is densely covered with blackish scales. Its **stipes** are 20–40 cm long, stout, brown at the base and green above. The **frond blade** is 4–45 cm long by 2–20 cm wide, dull to shiny green, thick and fleshy, and once-pinnate. Its **pinnae** are oblong to narrowly oblong, finely toothed around their margins and, generally, have blunt tips, although on some forms of the species they may be pointed. The **sori** are up to 1 cm long and do not extend to the margins. The shore spleenwort has a somewhat discontinuous distribution around the New Zealand coast. There are two distinct forms. One (*Blechnum obtusatum* subspecies *northlandicum*) occurs on the Kermadec and Three Kings Islands, and around the North Island where it is found from North Cape to northern Taranaki and the Bay of Plenty. The typical form (*B. obtusatum* subspecies *obtusatum*) occurs from Wellington, around South Island coastal regions, and on Stewart and the Chatham Islands. North of Oamaru it is rare on the east coast of the South Island. It is mainly found on coastal cliffs and rocks (where it often exposed to salt spray), or under coastal scrub. It also occurs on some of the sub-antarctic islands, in Australia and South America as well as some circum-antarctic islands of the Pacific. It is also known as paranako.

Asplenium obtusatum subspecies *northlandicum.*

Petako *Asplenium polyodon*

Petako is mainly an epiphytic fern, usually with long, drooping fronds that, on large plants, can be up to 1 m or more in length. It is a most handsome species and is found in moist forests throughout much of the country. Although its **rhizome** is described as 'shortly creeping' it generally forms small tufts or large clumps. Its dark brown **stipes** are 9–65 cm long. The **frond blades** are 15 cm to 1.2 m long, medium to deep green, shiny and simply pinnate. The **pinnae** are broadest at their bases and quite prominently toothed around their margins. Its **sori** are up to 2 cm long. Petako is found from the Kermadec and Three Kings Islands through the North, South and Stewart Islands and across to the Chatham Islands. It is common in lowland to montane forests, but is rare on the dry eastern side of the South Island. As well as growing as an epiphyte on trees and tree fern trunks, it also grows on rocks and on the ground. The petako is also known as peretao. This species occurs in Australia and is widespread in tropical regions from the Pacific islands to Madagascar.

ASPLENIACEAE

This is a distinct species that occurs only in southern regions. In some respects it is not dissimilar to *A. obtusatum*, having the thick and leathery fronds of that species, except that the pinnae are quite narrow and their margins are strongly and prominently toothed. It has a stout, tufted **rhizome** from which the 15–50 cm **stipes** arise. They have brownish bases and are green above. The **frond blade** is slightly drooping, 15–50 cm long by 8–20 cm wide, deep green with its upper surface dull or shiny, and simply pinnate. The narrow **pinnae** taper to long, pointed tips and the margins are regularly and deeply toothed. Its **sori** are up to 1 cm long and arranged in the herringbone pattern typical of most spleenworts. *Asplenium scleroprium* is found at the very south of the South Island, on Stewart Island and some of the muttonbird islands, and thence down to The Snares and Auckland Islands. On the mainland it occurs at Bluff and at Sandy Point Domain near Invercargill. It mainly grows on coastal cliffs and scrub, particularly where exposed to salt spray, or in coastal forest. Near Invercargill it also finds a habitat in exotic pine plantations.

Maidenhair spleenwort *Asplenium trichomanes*

This is a cosmopolitan species that occurs in the temperate regions of both hemispheres. The common name refers to the fact that the dead frond stalks remain after the leaflets (pinnae) have been shed, and not to its resemblance to *Adiantum*. It has a tufted **rhizome** and generally forms small clumps from 5–7 cm across. Its shiny dark brown to black **stipes** are 1–4 cm long, stiff and wiry. The **frond blades** are 4–20 cm long by 5–19 mm across, usually dark green and somewhat shiny, and simply pinnate. The **pinnae** are rounded to more or less oval. The **sori** form a herringbone pattern on the underside but, when mature, appear to cover the whole of the undersides of the pinnae. The maidenhair spleenwort occurs in the North and South Islands from coastal to subalpine regions. It is, perhaps, less commonly distributed in the North Island, occurring near Whangarei, in the King Country, Hawke's Bay and in the Wairarapa. In the South Island it is more widely distributed along the eastern side of the island. Although it grows on a variety of rock types including greywacke and mica-schist, it shows a definite preference for limestone and may be found in many limestone areas. It grows in open situations, in lightly shaded rock crevices and on rock bluffs.

Deparia petersenii is a fern with soft, deep green fronds, often found growing on the shady banks of creeks and streams. It has a rather stout, creeping **rhizome** and may form quite large colonies. Its pale brown **stipes** are 5–40 cm long. The narrowly triangular **frond blades** are 15–50 cm long by 6–25 cm wide, of a thin texture and twice-pinnate. Its **ultimate segments** are more or less oblong with blunt tips and slightly toothed around their margins. The **sori** are 1–3 cm long. On each segment the sori are arranged in herringbone fashion so that this species could be mistaken for an *Asplenium*. However, fine, scattered hairs on the frond blade show that it is not an *Asplenium*. *Deparia petersenii* occurs on the Kermadec Islands and in the North Island, where it is common from North Cape to the Waikato and Bay of Plenty, and then it is of scattered distribution along the west coast. In the South Island it occurs in north-western Nelson and then down the west coast as far south as Westport. It usually grows along shady stream banks, around forest margins, on grassy hillsides and under both native and naturalised scrub. Apparently, it is a comparatively recent introduction to New Zealand, not being recorded until 1906. Particularly in the far north, it is now common and appears to be gradually spreading farther southwards.

Southern lady fern *Diplazium australe*

This is often quite a large and handsome fern that, to the unwary, can masquerade as a spleenwort because its sori are arranged in herringbone fashion. The paired sori in a back-to-back arrangement help to distinguish it. It has a stout **rhizome** that can form a short, woody trunk. Its **stipes** are 15–80 cm long, stout and erect and brownish green. The deep green, broadly triangular **frond blade** is 25 cm to 1.2 m long by 20–90 cm wide, of a rather thin and delicate texture, and quite smooth. It is two- to three-times pinnate. Its **ultimate segments** are toothed around their margins. The numerous **sori** are 2–3 mm long and arranged in irregular pairs. In the North Island it is fairly common in lowland forests from Mangonui southwards but is absent from many eastern coastal areas. In the South Island southern lady fern is found in coastal areas from the Marlborough Sounds to Nelson and then down the west coast to Greymouth. It mainly grows around forest margins and along stream banks. Unfortunately, this fern is becoming less common because of forest clearance but it is still relatively common in some areas.

Smooth shield fern *Lastreopsis glabella*

This is a beautiful fern that is not difficult to recognise. Its fronds are quite distinctively shaped, being broadly triangular, while on the two main basal pinnae their two lowest branches are much longer than the others. It has an erect, tufted **rhizome** sometimes bearing the basal portions of the old stipes. Its usually reddish brown **stipes** are 6–30 cm long and are smooth apart from some scales at their bases. The **frond blades** are 10–35 cm long by 5–25 cm wide, deep green, dull to somewhat shiny and of a firm texture; three-times pinnate. The **ultimate segments** are narrow and toothed. Its **sori** are rather widely spaced and about halfway between the margin and the main vein. Smooth shield fern is distributed through the North, South, Stewart and Chatham Islands and is found in lowland forests. It often grows in drier forests but also occurs in moist forests, along streamsides and among rocks. This species is confined to New Zealand. It is closely related to *L. microsora*, which is distinguished by having creeping, not tufted, rhizomes.

Rough shield fern *Lastreopsis hispida*

Rough shield fern is very easily recognised by the coarse, bristly hairs on its stipes and midribs. It has quite finely divided, feathery fronds and is really a beautiful species. It has a far-creeping **rhizome** and, in some areas, forms quite large and conspicuous colonies. The **stipes** are 12–50 cm long and dark brown. Its **frond blades** are 18–50 cm long by 15–40 cm wide, three- to four-times pinnate, firm to rather harsh in texture, yellow-green to deep green and sometimes with a slight bronzy tint. The **ultimate segments** are narrow and sharply toothed. Its **sori** are rather large and numerous with one to each segment. The rough shield fern is widespread in the North Island in coastal to lower montane forests and in the South and Stewart Islands in coastal and lowland forests. It is usually uncommon in the drier eastern areas of the South Island. Although it is found in moist forests, it often appears to prefer drier slopes in the shadier parts of the forest. The rough shield fern is primarily a terrestrial species, but it does grow as a low epiphyte, particularly on the trunks of tree ferns. It also occurs in Australia. It is sometimes known as the hairy fern.

DRYOPTERIDACEAE

In contrast to *L. glabella*, this species has soft, pale green fronds and may be easily distinguished by its creeping (not tufted) rhizomes. Its **stipes** are 15–50 cm long and bear brownish scales and fine hairs, another point that distinguishes it from the smooth shield fern. The **frond blade** is 15–35 cm long by 10–25 cm wide, of firmish texture, smooth, pale to light green in colour and three- to four-times pinnate. Its **ultimate segments** are oblong and toothed around their margins. The **sori** are quite widely spaced, rather large and nearer to the margin than the main vein. *Lastreopsis microsora* occurs in the North, South and Chatham Islands. It is more common in the North Island while in the South Island it is more localised, occurring mainly in coastal regions as far south as northern Westland and Dunedin. It is usually found in coastal and lowland forests, especially along river and stream banks, particularly where the soil is of an alluvial nature. This species also occurs in Australia.

Velvet fern *Lastreopsis velutina*

As well as being a beautiful species, this fern is easily identified because of the soft, velvety feel of its fronds, which is due to a covering of minute reddish hairs. On its broadly triangular fronds the two lower-most secondary segments on each of the basal, primary pinnae are greatly length-ened to give the frond a distinctive shape, much more so than other members of the genus. In fact, they may be described as being five-angled. Its **rhizome** is tufted and  erect. The erect **stipes** are 15–40 cm long and covered with soft, brown hairs. The **frond blades** are 15–55 cm long by 15–45 cm wide and green or with a reddish brown tinge. The midribs of the fronds are so densely covered with soft, velvety hairs that they have a much darker appearance than the rest of the frond. Its oblong **ultimate segments** have blunt tips and have rather small and copious **sori**. The velvet fern is confined to the North and South Islands, usually in drier coastal and lowland forests. In the North Island it has a rather scattered distribution, while in the South Island it can be found from Cape Farewell down the eastern coast as far as Dunedin. As with the North Island its distribution is rather localised.

Black shield fern *Polystichum richardii*

Black shield fern is common throughout much of New Zealand and is fairly distinctive, usually because of the harsh nature of its fronds and their blackish green colour. It has a short and thick, tufted **rhizome** that is densely covered with dark brown scales. The **stipes** are 8–35 cm long and usually densely covered with deciduous scales. Its harsh and leathery **frond blades** are 10–50 cm long by 4–25 cm wide, their upper surfaces deep green to blackish green, paler beneath and two- to three-times pinnate. The **ultimate segments** are coarse and finely pointed. Its **sori** are one of its distinctive features, usually being quite large and before maturity they have prominent black discs in their centres, surrounded by pale margins. The black shield fern is found on the Three Kings Islands, in the North and South Islands, and on Stewart and the Chatham Islands. It is common in coastal to montane regions throughout the North Island; in the South Island from Nelson and Marlborough down the east to Invercargill, and is uncommon on Stewart Island. It usually grows in drier forests and scrub, on rocky banks, forest margins, and exposed coastal rocks. This species is also known as tutoke and shore shield fern. It is a very variable species and it is quite probable that it includes more than the one species.

Prickly shield fern *Polystichum vestitum*

This is a very handsome species that forms large and bold clumps of numerous dark green fronds. It attains its greatest luxuriance in the cooler mountain forests of the South and Stewart Islands. It has a short and stout **rhizome** that builds up to quite a large mass, and with age may even form a trunk up to 1 m or so tall. The **stipes** are 10–50 cm long and are densely clad with spreading, shiny scales that are dark brown with tawny margins. Its rather long and narrow **frond blades** are 20 cm to 1 m long by 6–25 cm wide; they are deep green and shiny with a harsh texture, and are twice-pinnate. The **ultimate segments** have sharply pointed teeth around their margins and they have three to eight **sori** per segment. Prickly shield fern occurs in lowland to montane forests throughout the North Island from the Hunua Ranges southwards, and in the South, Stewart and Chatham Islands. In the north it is mainly confined to montane regions and is not common north of Rotorua. In the South Island, as well as in forests, it also grows in scrublands, forest margins and in tussock grasslands where its presence often indicates that the area was once forested. The prickly shield fern is also common on some of the subantarctic islands, extending as far south as Macquarie Island. It is sometimes known as puniu.

Stipes.

107

Climbing shield fern is a very handsome and easily recognised fern that is quite distinctive. It is most commonly seen growing on tree fern trunks, although it also climbs on trees and occasionally on rocks. The fronds are scattered along its stout and far-creeping **rhizome**, which is covered with golden-brown scales. Its **stipes** are 10–65 cm long and are quite stout. The green to yellowish green **frond blade** is 10–50 cm long by 7–40 cm wide, and has a thick, leathery texture with a sheen on its smooth upper surface. It is two- to three-times pinnate. Its **ultimate segments** have blunt teeth around their margins. The large and rounded black **sori** are also one of its distinguishing characters. The climbing shield fern is found in lowland to montane forests throughout the North Island and is less common in the South Island, being confined to the moister forests and absent from dry eastern areas. It also occurs on Stewart and the Chatham Islands. Although principally an epiphyte or rupestral, it occasionally grows terrestrially, particularly on the fibrous mounds that accumulate around the bases of some trees. As well as New Zealand this species is quite widespread in other Southern Hemisphere countries including South America, South Africa and Australia. It is also known as the leathery shield fern.

Jointed fern *Arthropteris tenella*

This species has a juvenile form quite distinct from that of the adult, to the extent that it could almost be taken for a different species. It has a sparingly branched, far-creeping **rhizome** that climbs on rocks and trees. Its short **stipes** are 2–6 cm long and are usually quite widely spaced along the rhizome and are jointed near their bases. The **frond blades** are 10–40 cm long by 5–15 cm wide, dark green and thin but of a firm texture, simply pinnate. The **segments** taper to fine points and have slightly scalloped margins; they are distinctly stalked and noticeably jointed where they connect to the midribs. Its round **sori** are produced in a single row close to each margin. *Arthropteris tenella* is found on the Three Kings Islands, and in coastal and lowland forests of the North Island. In the South Island it grows in the Marlborough Sounds and north-west Nelson. It also occurs on the Chatham Islands. Juvenile forms often have simple, lance-shaped fronds about 3–6 cm long that are usually broadest above their middles. As well as in New Zealand, it occurs in Australia, Norfolk Island and New Caledonia.

New Zealand ladder fern *Nephrolepis* species

Although it is unlike any other species of native fern, the New Zealand ladder fern is sometimes confused with the introduced *N. cordifolia*, which has become naturalised in some parts of the North Island. Not only is *N. cordifolia* a generally larger fern but it also has fleshy, potato-like tubers on its roots, something which our native species does not produce. As yet our native species has not been given a specific botanical name and is simply known as *N.* species or sometimes as *N.* 'Thermal', indicating its habitat. It has short and erect **rhizomes** but produces new plants from stolons that can be quite wide-spreading. Its **stipes** are 3–15 cm long, slender, green to greenish brown and brittle. The narrow **frond blades** are 25–65 cm long by 2.5–6 cm wide, tending to arch over, and may have upwards of 50 pairs of pinnae. The **pinnae** are oblong with broad bases and have entire or shallowly toothed margins. Its **sori** are kidney-shaped and closer to the margins than the main veins of the segments. Apart from the Kermadec Islands, the ladder fern is confined to the North Island where it is found only on banks near the hot pools of thermal areas or in cracks in the warm ground. Outside New Zealand, the fern is found on Norfolk Island and possibly on other Pacific islands.

Coastal hardfern *Blechnum blechnoides*

A coastal species that is never found far beyond the influence of salt spray, this is a characteristic plant of coastal rocky areas. It has a stout, tufted **rhizome** that may be erect or inclined. The dark coloured **stipes** are 1–7 cm long. The **frond blades**, of **sterile fronds**, are narrow, 5–45 cm long by 1–4 cm wide; in exposed habitats they are spreading but in sheltered habitats more erect. They are a deep green and of a firm texture. There are 20 to 40 pairs of **pinnae**, the lower ones becoming much smaller. The **fertile fronds** are usually shorter with widely spaced pinnae. The coastal hardfern occurs around the coasts of the North Island from North Cape southwards but is absent from the eastern coastline. In the south it is found around the coasts of the South and Stewart Islands. It mainly grows on coastal cliffs, on slightly shaded overhangs, along stream banks or sometimes in the shelter of scrubby forest close to the shore. Along the actual shoreline it is often to be found where there is a little moisture seeping through the rocks. Along the eastern South Island its distribution may be quite local. It also occurs on the subantarctic Auckland and Campbell Islands. The coastal hardfern was formerly known as *B. banksii*, but is now known to be identical with the South American *B. blechnoides*. It could possibly be confused with *B. chambersii* but may be distinguished by its sterile pinnae being somewhat shorter and fleshier than those of *B. chambersii*.

111

Nini *Blechnum chambersii*

BLECHNACEAE

Nini is a common species in moist places and along stream banks in just about every area of moist forest. It has rather stout and erect **rhizomes** that occasionally extend into a short trunk. Its dark brown **stipes** are 1–5 cm long, firm and erect and scaly at their bases. The **frond blade** (of sterile fronds) is lance-shaped with a slightly curving outline, 15–50 cm long by 4–6 cm wide, light green when young, becoming dark green as it ages and has 15 to 40 pairs of **pinnae**. The pinnae are longest about the middle of the frond and, particularly at the base, gradually reduce to small, alternate lobes. Its **fertile frond** is usually shorter than the sterile, the **sori** completely covering the pinnae. Nini occurs through the North, South and Stewart Islands, usually being common in lowland and montane forests except for the drier parts of Canterbury and Otago. It also occurs on the Chatham and Auckland Islands. It ranges from sea level to 800 m, and is most commonly found along stream banks and in other moist or damp places. The nini is also known as lance fern and rereti. As well as in New Zealand, it occurs in Australia and some Pacific islands.

Peretao *Blechnum colensoi*

This is a very easily recognised species of hard fern that is quite unlike any other native species. It has broad, leathery fronds that may be simple and strap-shaped or, more often, irregularly and deeply divided into a number of large lobes. Peretao is found in the North, South and Stewart Islands, usually being fairly common in wet lowland and lower montane forests. In addition it occurs on the Chatham Islands and extends southwards to the Auckland Islands. In the North Island it grows from the Hokianga Harbour southwards while in the South Island it is common from north-western Nelson and down the western side, but is of only local occurrence on the dry eastern side from Marlborough to Otago. Peretao grows mainly on moist banks and rock faces, particularly along streamsides, often where there is seeping or dripping water and generally in dark places. It has a shortly creeping **rhizome** that may send out branching growths. Its black **stipes** are 6–25 cm long, stout and scaly at their bases. On sterile fronds, the **frond blades** (if undivided) are 10–35 cm long by 2.5–6 cm wide and (if divided) 25 cm to 1m long by 12–30 cm wide. They are dark green and have a sheen that is enhanced when they are wet. The **fertile fronds** are generally of a similar size with up to 10 pairs of pinnae. This species is also known as petako and Colenso's hard fern.

Crown fern *Blechnum discolor*

The crown fern is a common, and very handsome, species forming extensive colonies in the forest. Its stout **rhizomes** often form woody trunks up to 30 cm tall and, from their bases, they also produce stolons to produce new plants and extend the colony. **Stipes** of the sterile fronds are 5–20 cm long and scaly at their bases. The hard-textured, sterile **frond blades** are 20 cm to 1 m long by 5–16 cm wide and form an elegant, vase-shaped crown. They have 35 to 60 pairs of **pinnae**, their upper surfaces being bright green and lustrous while the undersurfaces are grey-green to slightly brownish and distinctly paler. **Fertile fronds** are usually somewhat longer than the sterile, and stand more erect in the centre of the crown. Not infrequently, fertile fronds may be observed on which the pinnae, close to the midrib, are partially sterile and then become fertile on their outer halves, to give the fronds a rather peculiar appearance. The crown fern is abundant in coastal to montane, open forests of the North, South, Stewart and Chatham Islands. It is particularly common in higher altitude forests and often grows to the exclusion of all other vegetation. It is also known as sword fern, piupiu and petipeti.

Coastal hardfern *Blechnum durum*

This is a coastal species that is confined to the south of the South Island, Stewart Island, the Chatham Islands and some of the subantarctic islands. It is never found far from the influence of the sea. In the South Island it occurs on the coast from near Okuru (a little south of the Haast River) and then southwards to about the Catlins River. It often forms dense colonies on coastal banks, and under coastal forest

and scrub. The stout **rhizomes** are erect, sometimes forming short trunks. Its **stipes** are 2–6 cm long and scaly at their bases. The sterile **frond blades** are generally longer and wider than those of *B. blechnoides*, being 15–60 cm long by 3–10 cm wide. They are deep green with shiny upper surfaces and are of a leathery texture. There are 20 to 40 pairs of **pinnae**, which have smooth margins and blunt tips. The **fertile fronds** are slightly smaller than the sterile and have very close-set **pinnae** that curve slightly upwards. They are some of the characters that distinguish it from *B. blechnoides*. The **sori** cover the whole undersurface of the fertile pinnae.

Climbing hard fern *Blechnum filiforme*

As well as being the only climbing hard fern, *Blechnum filiforme* is one of the few high-climbing ferns in New Zealand. It is also another species that has a juvenile form so completely different from the adult that the two could be mistaken for quite different species. The **juvenile form** creeps over the ground on slender **rhizomes** and often covers large areas including whatever may be in its path. Its **fronds** are on **stipes** 1–6 cm long and the **frond blade** is 5–25 cm long by 1–5 cm wide. The **pinnae** have blunt tips and are coarsely toothed around their margins. When the juvenile encounters a tree trunk it begins to climb and it is then that a most interesting transformation commences. As it climbs the trunk its fronds grow larger until they are about six times as large and attain their adult form. Their **stipes** are up to 10 cm long. The sterile **frond blades** are up to 60 cm long by up to 15 cm wide, green to dark green and they have a drooping habit. They have up to 30 pairs of **pinnae** with pointed tips and finely

toothed around their margins. The **fertile fronds** are as large as or slightly larger than the sterile and have very narrow **pinnae** that are almost thread-like. The climbing hard fern is endemic and occurs throughout the North Island and in the South Island in the Marlborough Sounds and north-west Nelson. It often ascends to great heights up trees. It is also known as thread fern.

Juvenile.

116

Creek fern *Blechnum fluviatile*

This is a most easily recognised fern: its spreading, long and narrow sterile fronds with rounded, deep green pinnae, and the fertile fronds, standing up from the centre of the crown with their short, upright pinnae, are sufficient identification. It has a stout and tufted **rhizome**. Its rather short **stipes** are 4–10 cm long and densely scaly. The sterile **frond blades** are 15–75 cm long by 2–6 cm wide, deep green and with 20 to 60 pairs of rounded to slightly oblong

pinnae. The sterile fronds radiate out from the crown and lie almost flat on the ground. The **fertile fronds** are equal to or slightly longer than the sterile, usually dark brown, and their **pinnae** are held almost parallel to the midrib. The creek fern is found in the North, South, Stewart and Chatham Islands. It ranges from sea level to 800 m, and usually occurs in damp lowland to montane forests, especially in moist and shaded areas, and may be common alongside streams. It also extends down to the subantarctic islands and occurs from Australia to Indonesia and Malaysia. The creek fern is also known as kiwakiwa and kiwikiwi.

Blechnum fraseri is a handsome and very distinct species that usually grows in large or small colonies of miniature tree ferns. Its **rhizome** is stoloniferous and each growing tip forms a slender and erect, woody trunk about the thickness of a finger and may be up to 1.5 m tall. The **stipes** are 8–20 cm long and on their upper parts have curiously toothed wings. The sterile **frond blades** are 15–40 cm long by 8–25 cm wide, dark

green and somewhat leathery. It is twice-pinnate and, in this respect, is the only native hard fern to have its fronds divided more than once. The **fertile fronds** are not too dissimilar to the sterile, usually having longer stipes and narrower secondary segments. The **sori** completely cover the undersides of the segments to the extent that the frond may appear to be dead or dying.

Blechnum fraseri is common in lowland forests from North Cape to Tauranga and the King Country. In the South Island it occurs from north-west Nelson to about Westport. It commonly grows in rather dry forest and sometimes covers quite extensive areas of the forest floor. It also occurs in New Guinea and south-eastern Asia.

Fertile frond.

118

Mountain kiokio *Blechnum montanum*

This is one of several species of hard fern that tend to have a quite similar appearance. Its rather thick **rhizomes** are shortly creeping. Its **stipes** are 8–25 cm long and have scattered, pale brown scales. The sterile **frond blades** are 14–45 cm long by 6–25 cm wide, deep green to bronzy-green and have 6 to 20 pairs of oblong to slightly curved **pinnae**, usually rather crowded, with the longest being at or below the middle of the frond. The pinnae have tapering tips, their margins are finely toothed and the lowermost pinnae are scarcely shorter than the others. The **fertile fronds** are about the same length as the sterile ones, but as they tend to stand erect they appear to be longer. Their pinnae are also held in upright position. The mountain kiokio is found in the North Island from Mount Pirongia southwards, and in the South and Chatham Islands. It usually grows in montane and subalpine regions, but in the south of the South Island it may come down to sea level. It occurs mainly in forests but also in subalpine scrub, grasslands and rocky areas. It also extends down to the subantarctic islands. The mountain kiokio replaces *B. novae-zelandiae* at higher altitudes, but there can be an intergradation of the two species.

119

BLECHNACEAE

Black hard fern is one of the smaller and more cryptic species that cannot be mistaken for any other. Its fronds are such a dark green that they appear to be almost black and that character, together with the very large terminal lobe of its frond, make it very easy to identify. It has a tufted **rhizome** that is semi-erect. Its **stipes** are 3–10 cm long and very scaly. The sterile **frond blades** are 5–20 cm long by 1.5–5 cm wide, spreading and tending to lie on the ground. They are unusual because of the greatly enlarged terminal lobe or pinna, and the lowermost pair of pinnae generally are more enlarged than the pair immediately above. The pinnae are coarsely toothed around their margins. It has few **fertile fronds** and they are equal to or longer than the sterile fronds. Their erect pinnae are few and widely spaced with the terminal one being very elongated. The black hard fern is found in lowland to montane forests in the western half of the North Island; in the South Island it can be found from north-western Nelson and the west coast to Fiordland; and it is found on Stewart Island. It usually grows on clay banks along streams, in pockets under tree roots and under very shaded overhangs. The fern always grows in very dark and gloomy situations, which, together with its blackish colour, mean it is not easily seen. Sometimes its fronds are further camouflaged when small mosses and liverworts grow on them.

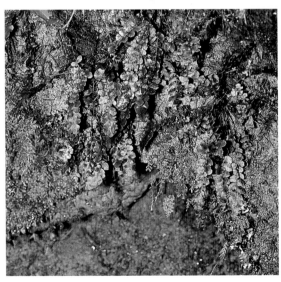

Kiokio *Blechnum novae-zelandiae*

A well-known and easily recognised species, kiokio is very common throughout most of the country except for the dry eastern areas of the South Island. In the moister parts of the country it dominates the landscape, clothing road banks and the sides of steep gullies with dense masses of its long and sweeping, palm-like fronds. The stout **rhizomes** are shortly creeping. Its **stipes** are 8–70 cm long and densely scaly with pale brown scales at their bases. The sterile

frond blades are 20 cm to 2.5 m long by 8–60 cm wide, bright green and with 10 to 50 pairs of crowded pinnae; those towards the base become progressively shorter and almost rounded. The **fertile fronds** either equal or are shorter than the sterile and they often have a few sterile pinnae at their bases. Kiokio occurs on the Kermadec and Three Kings Islands, and then through the North, South, Stewart and Chatham Islands. It is very common in lowland to montane areas, but is absent from much of the higher inland areas of the South Island as well as the dry eastern areas of Marlborough, Canterbury and Otago. In addition to its more obvious habitats it also grows in swampy areas and in scrublands. It will hybridise with one or two related species. Formerly, this species was known as *B. capense*. The kiokio is also known as horokio, common hard fern and palm-leaf fern.

Alpine hard fern *Blechnum penna-marina* subspecies *alpina*

BLECHNACEAE

This is perhaps the smallest native species of hard fern and, with the exception of the northern North Island, it is also quite ubiquitous. The alpine hard fern has creeping **rhizomes** and will eventually form extensive colonies. Its reddish brown **stipes** are 2–17 cm long, slender and wiry. The **fronds** are tufted along the rhizomes, erect, spreading or more or less flattened on the ground. The sterile **frond blades** reach 3–25 cm long by 6–15 mm wide, and are usually of a firm texture, dark green and simply pinnate. The **pinnae** arise in about 20 to 40 pairs (often alternating), mostly of equal length but reducing towards the base. **Blades** of fertile fronds are up to twice as long as the sterile fronds, with pinnae more widely spaced and often slightly curved upwards. The **sori** are copious and cover the whole undersurface of the pinna. The alpine hard fern occurs throughout the three main islands, on the Chatham Islands and down to the subantarctic islands, extending as far south as Macquarie Island. It is common in lowland to high alpine areas. In the North Island it is quite local from the Bay of Plenty northwards but is more common south of East Cape. In the South and Stewart Islands it is very common. It grows in open forest, scrub, open grasslands, moraines, herbfields and fellfields and ranges from sea level to 2000 m. In dry grasslands and the higher altitude habitats it is often quite dwarfed. *Blechnum penna-marina* subspecies *alpina* is the only form of this fern that is found in the Australasian region and it is also found in South America.

Triangular fern *Blechnum vulcanicum*

In spite of its name, *Blechnum vulcanicum* is no more common in volcanic areas than it is elsewhere. It is easily recognised by the general outline of its frond, which is wedge-shaped, with the lowermost pair of pinnae being the longest and distinctively curved downwards. The **rhizomes** are short and stout, and erect or inclined. Its pale yellowish brown **stipes** are 5–40 cm long and scaly at their bases. The dull green, sterile **frond blade** is 10–35 cm long by 4–12 cm wide, of a rather harsh texture and with 10 to 25 pairs of pinnae. Its **pinnae** have pointed or slightly blunt tips and wavy and minutely toothed margins. The **fertile fronds** are usually longer than the sterile, with longer stipes, and with the basal pair of pinnae quite prominently down-curved. The triangular fern is found in lowland to higher montane forests of the North, South and Stewart Islands, and on the Chatham Islands. In the North Island it is very local from the Bay of Islands to the Bay of Plenty, but fairly common from there to Wellington. In the South Island it is common in lowland to montane areas, often on road banks, banks in open forest and on rock faces. It is more local, or absent, in the drier parts of Marlborough, Canterbury and Otago. It is also known as the mountain hard fern and korokio. The triangular fern also occurs in Australia, New Guinea, Indonesia, the Philippines and some Pacific islands.

Rasp fern *Doodia australis*

Rasp fern is more common in the northern parts of the country and is distinguished by its rather harsh-textured fronds, sori that are paired and parallel to the main vein of the pinna and the prominent rosy-red of its young fronds, particularly in the spring. It has a tufted **rhizome** from which stolons grow to create a colony. Its blackish brown **stipes** are 2–25 cm long and more or less scaly towards their bases. The **frond blades** are 11–60 cm long by 1–10 cm wide, dark green and rough to the touch, and with 20 to 50 pairs of pinnae and a very long, drawn-out terminal pinna. The **pinnae** are longest towards the middle of the frond and become much smaller towards the base; their margins are sharply toothed. **Sori** occur in a single row either side of, and parallel to, the main vein of the pinna. The rasp fern is common in coastal and lowland areas, occurring on the Kermadec and Three Kings Islands, in the North Island and in the north of the South Island. In the North Island it is common from North Cape to the Waikato and Bay of Plenty and then more scattered in coastal localities southwards to Wellington. In the South Island it is confined to coastal locations around the Marlborough Sounds and in north-west Nelson. It is also known as pukupuku and is endemic to New Zealand.

Pacific azolla *Azolla filiculoides*

Not only is this unfern-like plant a fern, but it is also free-floating on water and, apart from little rootlets hanging in the water, does not root into anything solid. The plants are about 3 x 3 cm and usually form extensive green to reddish brown mats, or colonies, on the surface of the water. Their **fronds** are irregularly branched and have secondary branches, all of which are densely overlapping. The frond **lobes** are ovate and have blunt tips. The **rootlets** are up to 7 cm long and are not branched. Apparently, fertile plants capable of producing spores are rare so that virtually all reproduction is vegetative. Plants are transferred to new habitats by water fowl, such as ducks, which probably carry small pieces of them on their feet. The Pacific azolla is found in the North and South Islands in ponds, small lakes and slow-moving streams. In the northern part of the North Island it occurs in lowland to montane regions from about Dargaville southwards. The introduced, and rather similar, *A. pinnata* (can be distinguished by having branched rootlets) has largely replaced the native species in Northland and may also occur as far south as the Waikato region. In the South Island the Pacific azolla largely occurs in lowland eastern districts from Nelson to about the Clutha River. The fern is also known as karearea, retoreto or returetu.

Glossary

Acute sharply pointed.

Alternate placed singly along each side of an axis or midrib, not in pairs.

Blunt not pointed at the ends.

Bristly hairs hairs having pointed tips.

Bulbil a bud produced vegetatively on a stem or frond, and capable of growing into a new plant. See gemma.

Caudex the stem of a tree fern.

Cone a term used for the aggregated fructifications of clubmosses.

Crown the growing point of an upright rhizome, or trunk, and usually producing a ring or circle of fronds.

Emergent trees or tree ferns that tower above the general canopy area of a forest and are usually scattered so that they appear more as individuals or groups of individuals.

Endemic native to only a particular country or region.

Epiphyte a plant that grows or perches upon another plant but is not organically connected to it; adjective epiphytic.

Frond a leaf, especially those of ferns.

Gemma a small asexual, reproductive structure (particularly of ferns, liverworts and mosses) that becomes detached from the parent and develops into a new individual; plural gemmae.

Glabrous without hairs of any kind; smooth.

Hair a thin and delicate outgrowth consisting of one cell, or a single row of cells; it may be branched.

Indigenous native to a country, or region, but not necessarily confined to that country or region.

Indusium an outgrowth of tissue more or less covering the sorus in some ferns.

Jointed breaking easily at particular points.

Lamina the flattened part, or leafy part, of a frond usually borne at the end of the stipe.

Lateral attached to or borne from the side.

Linear very narrow with parallel margins.

Lobe a recognisable, but not separated, segment of a frond or frond part, particularly when rounded.

Margin the edge or border of a frond or frond segment.

Midrib the main central vein of a frond or main division of a frond.

Opposite a pair of frond segments that arise at the same level on opposite sides of a midrib.

Ovate a frond, or frond segment, that is broadest at its lower end and is generally egg-shaped.

Pakihi open, barren land; used especially for flat, badly drained areas (particularly alluvial, terraced land). Mostly on the western side of the South Island, pakihis usually have a characteristic vegetation of shrubby plants, rush-like plants, tangle fern and clubmosses.

Pinna a division, especially a primary division, of a divided frond (or leaf). Usually expressed as primary, secondary or tertiary according to the number of times that a frond is divided; plural pinnae.

Pinnate having the blade of a frond divided as far as the midrib or rachis so that there are separate lobes or divisions.

Pinnule the ultimate division of a pinna.

Primary pinna the principal segment of a divided frond; such a segment may be further divided into secondary and tertiary pinnae.

Rachis (or rhachis) the main stem of a frond blade.

Rhizome an underground stem usually spreading more or less horizontally (creeping), or short and erect and sometimes extending above ground to form a short, erect trunk.

Round-ended when the segments of a frond blade have rounded ends or tips.

Rupestral growing on rock.

Scale a small, flattened, often dry and membranous outgrowth from the stipes, rachis or frond blade that is often leaf-like.

Secondary pinna the principal segment of a primary pinna that is again divided. It may again be divided into tertiary pinnae.

Sessile tapering to the base but lacking any obvious stalk or stipe.

Sorus a cluster of two or more sporangia on the margin or underside of a lamina or frond blade. Usually a sorus has a characteristic shape or form.

Sporangium a sac or capsule that contains spores.

Spore a single-celled reproductive unit, similar in function to the seed of a flowering plant.

Sporophyll a modified, more or less leaf-like structure that bears the sporangia on plants such as clubmosses and fork ferns. On clubmosses they are often aggregated into a strobilus.

Sterile frond a frond that does not produce sporangia.

Stipe the stalk from which the frond blade is produced; plural stipes.

Strobilus a cone-like structure containing reproductive organs, as in lycopods or clubmosses; plural strobili.

Tertiary pinna the principal segment of a secondary pinna which is again divided; it may be again divided into quaternary pinnae.

Whorl an arrangement of three or more branches arising at the same level around a stalk or stem; adjective whorled.

Wing a thin and, usually, narrow portion of a frond blade bordering the stem or midrib.

Further reading

Allan, H.H., 1961, *Flora of New Zealand*, Vol. 1, Government Printer.

Brownsey, P.J. and Smith-Dodsworth, J.C., 2000, *New Zealand Ferns and Allied Plants*, David Bateman.

Crowe, A., 1994, *Which Native Fern?*, Viking.

Dobbie, H.B. and Crookes, M., 1952, *New Zealand Ferns*, Whitcombe and Tombs.

Index

Notes

Notes

Notes

Notes